CURRICULUM
LINKS

ages
5–7

The seaside

Suzanne Kirk

Credits

Author
Suzanne Kirk

Editor
Roanne Charles

Assistant editor
Jon Hill

Series designer
Lynne Joesbury

Designer
Catherine Mason

Illustrations
Bethan Matthews

Cover photograph
© Taxi/Getty Images

Photographic symbols
Music and history © Stockbyte.
Geography © Photodisc, Inc.

Published by Scholastic Ltd,
Villiers House,
Clarendon Avenue,
Leamington Spa,
Warwickshire
CV32 5PR
Printed by Bell & Bain Ltd, Glasgow
Text © Suzanne Kirk
© 2004 Scholastic Ltd
1 2 3 4 5 6 7 8 9 0   4 5 6 7 8 9 0 1 2 3

Visit our website at www.scholastic.co.uk

British Library Cataloguing-in-Publication Data
A catalogue record for this book is available from
the British Library.

ISBN 0-439-97121-7

Contents

Acknowledgements

Photographs
page 5 © Eyewire
page 19 © Nova Developments
pages 26 and 32 © Ikon Imaging
page 30 © Bubbles/Gary Buss
page 40 © Ingram Publishing, © Image Club
page 45 © Popperfoto/Reuters,
© Getty Images/Gary Buss
page 47 © Photodisc, Inc.
page 57 © Getty Images/Mel Yates
page 58 © Bubbles/Lucy Tizzard

Introduction

This book provides suggestions and activities covering separate areas of the curriculum that, as a whole, create an exciting and motivating topic to raise children's awareness of the seaside past and present. The book considers the delights of holidays by the sea today and in the past; highlights physical and human features, making comparisons with the local area; and explores some of the typical sounds of a seaside location.

The Seaside brings together aspects of geography, history and music. It will help you to present an interesting topic at Key Stage 1 over a number of weeks, enabling the children to develop mapwork skills, find out about and discuss different places, share experiences, discover ways of investigating the past and become involved in musical exploration.

Generally, the activities in each section follow on progressively. Section 1 investigates when and why we have holidays. In section 2, the children discuss the features of seaside holidays. Section 3 compares the children's local area with a seaside locality. In section 4, the children investigate seaside holidays of the past, and section 5 looks beyond the British Isles to holidays abroad. Section 6 is the music section, where the activities build up to a performance of a class composition. The music activities can take place throughout the topic as appropriate.

What subject areas are covered?

This book covers the QCA Schemes of Work geography unit 4, 'Going to the seaside', history unit 3, 'What were seaside holidays like in the past?' and music unit 7, 'Exploring timbre, tempo and dynamics', in this case through the stimulus of the seaside.

Most children, especially those who live away from the sea, are curious about and enchanted by this fascinating environment. Visits to the seaside are always eagerly anticipated. Those living close to the sea are fortunate to experience the different landscapes of town, countryside and seaside as they grow up.

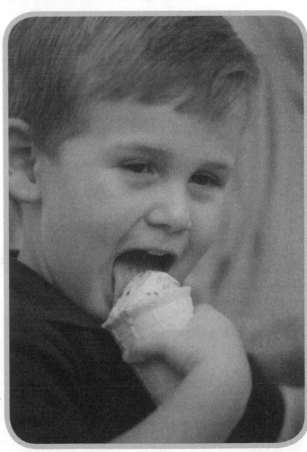

Mapwork, photographs, artefacts, stories and music can have the effect of bringing the seaside to the classroom where a visit to the coast is not possible. The early activities of this book help to make the distinction between 'normal' days and holidays, then between holidays in different environments. The seaside becomes a focus in both past and present times. The music activities, which build up to the performance of a class composition portraying the seaside, can be inserted into the topic at appropriate times. Music activity 1 relates directly to activity 5 in section 1; the other activities can develop with the children's knowledge and awareness as the topic proceeds.

Teaching specific subject areas through a topic

While it is important to distinguish between the separate subject areas of geography, history and music, natural links can be difficult to ignore and are extremely useful in relating one area of work with another. One subject focus can provide an opportunity to explore in another field.

A carefully planned topic can meld together prescribed areas of the curriculum to create interesting learning experiences appropriate to the class. Topic-based work presents a whole picture that motivates children and encourages their enthusiasm.

Getting started

Get to know the nearest seaside resorts to your locality – the places families might go to for a day out. Collect brochures, postcards, guide books and memorabilia, as well as shells, driftwood and pebbles to build up a seaside atmosphere in the classroom. Check out museums, galleries and libraries for additional information and arrange for a suitable individual to talk to the children about their childhood memories of seaside visits. Try to find a dramatic or evocative print or painting perhaps by a local artist to use as a stimulus for the topic. Collect music and sounds that evoke the essence of being by the sea.

Involving parents and carers

Involving parents and carers is a useful strategy in helping to motivate children during their topic work on the seaside. This topic is a particularly useful one, as most parents/carers and grandparents will enjoy sharing their memories of childhood times at the seaside and hearing the children describe their experiences of visits.

At the beginning of the topic, prepare a letter to parents and carers outlining the areas of work in which their children will be involved. Encourage them to share their childhood memories with the children as well as listening to them as they report on the progress of the topic. Take this opportunity to ask for the loan of photographs, artefacts and souvenirs relating to seaside activities in the past. Explain that if possible the children should bring to school a photograph of themselves enjoying a recent seaside holiday.

Perhaps a parent/carer would be willing to take photographs or video footage, or record sounds on a visit to a familiar seaside location. Provide a list that includes images of physical features and buildings characteristic of the resort, as well as people enjoying typical seaside activities.

Promise parents a special *Seaside* event at the end of the topic, which could be an exhibition of the children's work with a performance of the musical exploration.

Introducing the topic to children

Children living inland for whom visits to the coast are infrequent, will be especially delighted to have a seaside atmosphere brought to them in the classroom. Children within easy reach of the sea will appreciate the opportunity to contribute useful first-hand knowledge and experiences.

Present the topic as an exciting one for both the children and yourself, with lots of things to look forward to. Create a sense of fun and discovery. Explain that they will be using different ways to find out about the seaside; looking at maps and books, listening to stories and music. Mention any visits to be made or visitors who will come to talk to the children. Point out the three aspects of the topic: finding out about the landscape and what people do at the seaside, which is geography; discovering what the seaside was like in the past – history; exploring the sounds of the seaside – music.

Starting points

It might be useful to find out what responses the topic of the seaside prompts in the children. Do they go to the seaside often, once a year, or even at all? What do they look forward to doing and seeing when they get there? What do they know about already or what would they like to know about? Ask the children what they think they might find out during a topic about the seaside. What would they like to discover?

Fieldwork opportunities

It is helpful if the children have already been out and about in the neighbourhood of the school, looking at the uses of land and the types of buildings common to their area.

Depending on the proximity to the coast, a visit to the seaside would enable the children to make direct comparisons at first-hand of this environment with their own. They could observe and identify physical features, buildings and uses of land that are characteristic of a seaside environment.

Resources required

General

☐ Illustrations, paintings, prints, postcards, photographs, video film and so on of seaside locations, especially those with which the children are familiar

☐ Still and video images showing specific buildings and identifiable land use at seaside places

☐ Guidebooks, maps and other promotional material provided by tourist information services for British resorts; travel brochures for seaside locations abroad

☐ Picture books, stories and poems relating to the seaside

☐ A range of material relating to festivals, seasons and the different landscapes of town and countryside

☐ A camera

For mapwork

☐ Aerial photographs of the school's locality and of seaside places

☐ A satellite photograph of the British Isles

☐ A large, simple map of the British Isles

☐ Atlases

☐ A globe

Collections

☐ A group of items to represent a school day and a 'holiday' from school. See section 1, activity 1

☐ Historical artefacts relating to the seaside of the past: souvenirs, postcards, posters, tickets, advertising material and so on

☐ Items to create a seaside atmosphere, such as beach toys, shells, pieces of driftwood, holiday wear, swimwear, sunglasses, sun hats, sunscreen bottles, sunshade, windbreak

For music activities

☐ A collection of instruments

☐ Recording equipment

☐ Recordings of typical sounds of town, countryside and seaside

☐ Pieces of music to represent town, countryside and seaside

■ Songs with a seaside theme

Make use of services and resources provided by local and seaside museums and libraries. If possible, arrange for an adult to visit the class to talk to the children and answer questions about his or her seaside experiences as a child.

Section 1

Visiting different places

FOCUS

HISTORY
■ holidays and when we have them
■ recalling information from the past

HISTORY

GEOGRAPHY
■ different places for holidays
■ using geographical vocabulary
■ mapwork
■ conducting a survey

GEOGRAPHY

Preparation for section 1

Be aware that you will need to be sensitive towards children who do not have holidays. This section focuses on holidays in the British Isles. (Section 5 deals with travelling further afield.)

ACTIVITY 1

WHAT ARE HOLIDAYS?

HISTORY

Learning objective

To recognise that holidays are different from ordinary days.

Resources

A collection of artefacts in a box and two trays for sorting; paper; pencils and crayons.

Preparation

Collect some everyday objects to represent a typical school day, such as an item of PE clothing, an exercise book, a set of crayons, a lunch box, a musical instrument and a ruler; and also to represent a day's holiday, for example one or two toys, casual clothing, a book and leaflet about a local attraction. Put both sets of items together in a box.

Activity

As it is probably the beginning of a new term, ask the children how they feel about being back at school. How many people are glad to be back? Who wishes the holidays were longer? Encourage the children to distinguish between 'holidays' and 'normal' days. Normally they attend school during the week, but from time to time they have holidays from school. How do they feel about school days compared with holidays? Do they feel any different?

Take the children through a school day. When do they get up? What do they do next? Talk about getting ready and the urgency of being on time. Then there is the routine of the school day. Emphasise the enjoyment and benefits of coming to school, learning new skills, meeting friends and so on. What do the children do when they get home after school? Do they like to play? Do they have a meal? What activities can they fit in before bedtime?

Then compare a day of the holidays. Do the children get up at the same time? Perhaps they go to spend a day or two with a carer or relative. Do they have to hurry about as much? Do they wear different clothes? Do they sometimes go on visits to the park, the shops, another town, the countryside? Perhaps they go away for several days. Are meal times different? Do the children have more time for play? Do they continue to do some of the things that they do at school, such as reading, writing and drawing? Do they go to bed at a different time?

Tell the children you have a box of everyday items of which some are used on school days and others when on holiday. Ask some children to take out objects one at a time and decide whether they would be likely to be used on a school day or on holiday. Do all the children agree? Perhaps some items could fit in both collections – in which case, find something similar, so that a book or craft item, for example, can be represented in both groups.

Point out that it is pleasant to have holidays to look forward to, but at the same time it is important and enjoyable to attend school to learn new things.

Recording
Ask the children to illustrate four events or activities in a school day and four events in a holiday from school. Point out that this should just be a day when they are not at school, rather than a day of a holiday when they are away from home. Some children might like to pair the events, perhaps according to different times of the day.

Differentiation
Children:
■ recognise differences between a school day and a holiday, recording with drawings
■ understand that there are differences between a school day and a holiday; make comparisons through drawings, words and phrases
■ describe differences between school days and holidays, comparing equivalent incidents during a day and recording details in drawings, words and phrases

Plenary
Discuss the children's work and comment on some differences between school days and holidays. Do the children generally agree? Remind them that there are things to look forward to about returning to school as well as looking forward to the holidays.

Display
Make a temporary arrangement of the everyday objects collected, with appropriate labels. Include the children's work as part of the display.

ACTIVITY 2

WHEN DO WE HAVE HOLIDAYS?

HISTORY

Learning objective
To know that there are certain parts of the year when holidays tend to take place.

Resources
A long sheet of paper for a timeline; photocopiable page 16; coloured pens; pencils and crayons; books about seasons and festivals.

Preparation
Be aware of the religious differences among the children and include religious festivals from different faiths in the discussion. Plan a timeline on a large sheet of paper (which can become

Visiting different places

a wall display), perhaps indicating main divisions with faint pencil marks. Base the timeline on the school year, starting with the beginning of the autumn term. If appropriate, indicate the months by their initial letter, otherwise just the seasons (see photocopiable page 16).

Activity
Ask the children to tell you when they have long holidays from school. They should be able to say that there are long holidays from school for Christmas, for Easter and for a summer break. Discuss what is celebrated at Christmas and Easter, and explain why there are holidays at these times in this country. Ask the children if they celebrate other festivals during the Christmas period, for example Divali or Hanukkah. Ask if there are any other holidays where special events are celebrated. Can the children tell you in which seasons of the year these holidays fall? Why do the children have a long holiday in the summer? Talk about the weather being warmer and the longer hours of daylight, so that time can be spent out of doors.

Show the horizontal line you have drawn to begin the timeline. Explain that this line will represent a school year, and on it you will mark the main holidays. Show that the line starts with the beginning of the school year, in September, and ends with the summer holidays. If appropriate, ask the children to recite the months of the year with you, using their initial letters to help.

Ask the children to help you locate the school holidays on the timeline. Start by recalling the last holiday the children had from school. Was it Christmas, Easter or the long summer break? Write in the holiday in the appropriate place and talk about the time of the year when it falls. Is it winter, spring or summer? Next, work out the positioning of the other main holidays and discuss the seasons in which they occur. Point out that the distinction between seasons is not easy to make, as spring blends into summer and so on.

Remind the children what is celebrated by Christians at Christmas and Easter. Discuss an appropriate symbol to include on the timeline to represent each holiday – perhaps a star or Christmas tree for Christmas, an egg or a cross for Easter and the sun for the summer holiday.

Find out what the children associate the summer holiday with. Is it going to the seaside, staying with relatives, staying at home and doing special things, having more time to play?

Recording
Use photocopiable page 16. Children should recognise the framework of the timeline, which has been discussed as a class. Make sure they understand that the letters represent the months and where the holidays fit in. Ask the children to draw their own symbols to represent each of the holidays, as well as small pictures to represent the seasons. Let them use reference books where necessary. Consider the inclusion of other important festivals and ask the children to indicate when their birthday is in relation to the holidays.

Differentiation
Children:
■ are aware that holidays take place at certain times of the year, adding to a timeline with help
■ are aware of the parts of the year when holidays take place and their relationship with religious festivals, recording information on a timeline
■ begin to understand the relationship between holidays and religious festivals, and seasons, recording detailed information on a timeline.

Plenary
Recall the relationship between holidays and religious festivals. Let the children ask each other questions to share the information they have recorded on their timelines, for example: *In which season do we have our Easter holiday? Which holiday do we have in December?*

Display
Arrange the timeline where it can be viewed and discussed, together with pictures and information about celebrations at different times of the year.

GEOGRAPHY   HISTORY

ACTIVITY 3

WHERE HAVE YOU BEEN?

Learning objectives
To name different places; to recall information from their past.

Resources
Pictures and postcards showing contrasts between towns, countryside and seaside places; photocopiable page 17; board or large sheet of paper; pencils and crayons.

Activity
Begin by talking about how exciting it is to visit somewhere for a day or a longer holiday, whether it is a place far away or close by. Perhaps tell the children about a low-key holiday you have enjoyed, such as staying with a friend in a different part of the country. Encourage children to tell you where they have been on holiday or a day trip. Compile a list. Briefly discuss some of the places as the list grows. Try to ensure there are examples of the three types of place – towns, countryside and seaside – in the list.

Discuss ways of grouping the places. The children might suggest splitting the list into places nearby and those where they need to travel by plane or boat to get there. Ask the children to show by putting up their hands whether they travelled by car, bus, train, plane or boat to reach their last holiday destination. Make some generalisations, such as: *Most people travelled by car, No one went by train.*

Go through the list and identify with a coloured pen those holiday places which are by the sea. Ask the children to suggest a symbol to represent the seaside (perhaps a representation of waves or a bucket and spade). Then identify those places which are towns; use a symbol to represent a building. Finally, pick out any places in the countryside and ask the children to think of a suitable symbol, for example a tree. The children should have little problem noticing which is the most popular type of holiday venue.

Recording
Provide the children with photocopiable page 17. Explain that in the shapes they can show the types of places where people like to go on holiday – by the sea, in a town, in the countryside. Ask the children to write the names of some of the places from the class list on the lines and draw appropriate illustrations or symbols inside the circles.

Differentiation
Children:
■ name and describe a holiday place, grouping places pictorially
■ are aware that there are different types of places for holidays, using symbols to group according to simple criteria
■ understand that there are differences between holiday places, using appropriate symbols to group according to simple criteria.

Plenary
Point out that people often like to visit places that are very different from where they live, perhaps the seaside if they live far from the coast, or the countryside if they live in a town.

Display
Begin a display to represent the three distinctive areas of town, countryside and seaside.

1

GEOGRAPHY

HISTORY

ACTIVITY 4

USING A MAP

Learning objectives
To locate familiar holiday places on a map of the British Isles; to recall details from their past.

Resources
Large map of the British Isles; atlases; satellite photograph showing the British Isles from space; small coloured stickers; coloured pens or pencils; photocopiable page 18.

Preparation
Find appropriate maps and atlases, which should be as simple as possible. If necessary, draw and cut out a large outline of the British Isles to use with the children. Mark with a sticker the town or village where the children live. Also mark it on page 18 before photocopying it.

Activity
Show the children a large map of the British Isles. Explain that this map represents the part of the Earth where they are. It has been made small so that we are able to see the whole of it, as it might be seen from space. Show the children the satellite photograph to help them understand that a map represents the shape of the country. On the large map, distinguish the land and the sea. Trace the coastline with a finger and explain that this is the point where the land meets the sea. Help the children to identify England, Scotland, Wales and Ireland.

Find the nearest seaside place and other coastal resorts the children might have visited. Use coloured stickers to mark the location of these seaside places, and write in their names.

Talk about the places the children have visited to enjoy the countryside and use a different coloured sticker to identify these locations. Perhaps talk about the Lake District, the Downs, the West Highlands, the Brecon Beacons. As these tend to cover larger areas than the seaside resorts, you may want to use three or four stickers to represent this.

Finally, locate any towns or big cities that have been visited, using another colour. Include a nearby interesting town the children might have visited in this group.

Organise the class into groups with enough atlases for one between two. Direct them to a suitable map so that they can help each other find the places that have been discussed. Move among the groups to stimulate their collaboration.

Recording
Provide the children with photocopiable page 18. If necessary, remind them of the parts representing land and sea and help them to locate and label the place where they live. Ask them to refer to the large map or an atlas to find the holiday places mentioned by the class, then, by looking carefully, mark them on their own map. Tell them to use different colours to represent towns, countryside and seaside. Show the children how this might be done by looking for easily identifiable features on each map: *Skegness is on this bulge of the coastline. I must find the same bulge on the small map and mark Skegness with a small dot. The Lake District covers a large part of the country so I can use a green colour to shade in this area.* Remind the children to choose different colours for each type of holiday place and explain what these mean in a key.

Differentiation
Children:
■ use a map to identify places and with help mark these on an individual map
■ use maps to identify familiar places, marking these accurately on an individual map
■ understand that maps are used to represent features of the Earth; identify places and mark these accurately on an individual map.

Plenary
Using their maps (photocopiable page 18), ask the children to identify seaside, town and countryside places referring to the colour coding they have used.

Display
Develop the display begun in activity 3. Include the large map with a key and/or the children's maps. Link these, by position or with thread/tape, with the work from activity 3.

GEOGRAPHY

HISTORY

ACTIVITY 5

TOWN–COUNTRYSIDE–SEASIDE

Learning objectives
To use geographical vocabulary; to represent pictorially information about different holiday places; to recall experiences to answer questions about holidays.

Resources
Pictures of town, countryside and seaside scenes; guidebooks and leaflets of a range of places to visit; photocopiable page 17; pencils and crayons; board or flip chart.

Preparation
A few days before this activity, ask the children to bring in a photograph of themselves on holiday. Ask them to try to find a snapshot that will give a clue to others as to whether the place is at the seaside, in the country or in a town or city.

Activity
Write three headings on the board: *town, countryside, seaside*. Choose one, perhaps the seaside, to start with and ask the children to suggest why people like to go there for their holidays. List the suggestions under the heading: sand, sea, dunes, beach huts, deck chairs, swimming, arcades, funfairs, piers, cliffs, seaside games, boat trips, rock pools and so on. Let the children look at the pictures and promotional leaflets as prompts and to identify features some of them might not have experienced. Move on to discuss the countryside, listing features such as hills, mountains, rivers, valleys, farms, fields, animals, walking, footpaths, stiles, outdoor games, camping. Finally, ask the children what attractions towns and cities provide and include shops, museums, sports facilities, cafés, cinemas, castles and so on.

In groups, encourage the children to show each other their photographs. Ask them to decide whether the holidays were at the seaside, in the town or in the countryside. Help them to identify clues like cliffs, an interesting town skyline or a good view across the landscape.

Recording
On photocopiable page 17, ask the children this time to draw symbols to represent activities enjoyed in each type of holiday place. Encourage them to include as many ideas as they can in each circle and to write key words, rather than names of places, on the lines.

Differentiation
Children:
■ use geographical vocabulary and represent information about holiday places pictorially
■ use a range of geographical vocabulary and detailed illustrations to give information about different holiday places
■ understand and use a wide range of geographical vocabulary, giving detailed pictorial information about contrasting holiday places.

1

Visiting
different
places

Plenary
Share the children's photographs. Ask the children to tell each other what clues told them about the places in the pictures.

Display
Add promotional leaflets and books, and the children's photographs if appropriate, to continue the town–countryside–seaside display.

ACTIVITY 6

WHERE HAVE OTHER PEOPLE BEEN ON HOLIDAY?

GEOGRAPHY

Learning objective
To devise and conduct a survey, using ICT to collate the results.

Resources
Computers and appropriate software; board or flip chart; paper; pencils and crayons.

Preparation
Decide on an appropriate method of carrying out the survey, which classes will be involved, when the children will complete the questionnaires and if they will be answered at school or at home. Consider the timescale: planning, answering the questions, sorting the information, drawing conclusions. Create a data file to receive the information the children collect from the survey.

Activity
Part 1 – planning the survey
Suggest that it would be interesting to know where other people have been for their holidays, perhaps children in other classes. It would also be interesting to know which place was the most popular for holidays. Ask the children how they could find out. They will probably suggest asking questions. Consider the best way of asking questions and recording the answers. Point out that it is easy to forget what people have said, especially if you are asking the same questions of several people. If necessary, prompt the children to think of conducting a written survey. Find out if the children are aware of any surveys their parents have taken part in, perhaps to find out about methods of recycling or their favourite supermarket/coffee/TV programme.

Discuss how the survey will be organised. Talk about preparing a set of questions that can be answered easily and quickly. Emphasise that a written survey like this is useful as the questions are standard and can be asked quickly, and the information can be stored until it is ready to be studied.

Guide the children towards a particular format for the questionnaire. This could be a simple list of popular holiday places with boxes to tick. Ask the children which places should be included in the survey. They will probably suggest those mentioned in previous activities. Draw a basic framework on the board to help the children see the form the survey might take. Consider:
■ a title
■ a polite request explaining the reason for the survey
■ instructions on how to complete it
■ places to include
■ adding some lines so that respondents can fill in favourite places that have not been included in the list

■ indicating when the survey should be returned
■ whether it is useful for people to give their names and/or ages
■ how the respondents can show which place is their favourite.
Write in some names of the holiday places on the survey sheet. Include at least two towns or cities, two countryside areas, and two seaside places.

Part 2 – distributing the questionnaires
Make arrangements with the teachers of any classes taking part in the survey. It might be possible for the participants to answer the questions as part of their class work.

Part 3 – analysing the questionnaires
Appoint a group of children to collect and store the survey sheets until required. Talk to the class about how the information collected can be used. Discuss ideas for ways of counting the ticks, perhaps using a master tally chart.
  Help the children to enter the information into the data file you have created. Print out different presentations of the findings, which should include graphs and comparisons of the numbers of visitors to town, country and seaside locations.

Part 4 – discussing the results of the survey
What are the children's first reactions? Is there an obviously favourite place where people have enjoyed a holiday? What are the top three holiday places? Which places were visited by only a few people? Are seaside holidays the most popular? Talk about the usefulness of a graph and how it clearly displays the information that was originally on lots of pieces of paper.

Holiday survey

We are finding out where people like to go on holiday in the British Isles. Please tick the places you have visited and perhaps add some others. Put a star by your favourite place (one only).

Holiday places	Please tick	Please star (one only)
Skegness		
London		
Yorkshire Dales		
Edinburgh		
Norfolk Broads		
Pembrokeshire Coast		

Recording
Help the children to compose and print out statements that explain the results of the survey. Ask the children to write a paragraph to explain their part in the survey.

Differentiation
Children:
■ take part in conducting a class survey and with help collate some of the answers using ICT
■ make suggestions and take part in preparing and conducting a class survey, using ICT to collate and demonstrate the results
■ understand the value of a survey, make suggestions and take part in conducting a class survey; use ICT proficiently to collate and demonstrate results.

Plenary
Discuss the usefulness of the survey and comment on the information collected. Ask the children what they have learned. Are any of the findings surprising? What have they discovered about holidays and holiday places that they did not know before the survey took place?

Display
Present the information obtained from the questionnaire together with the children's explanations on how the survey was conducted. If possible, arrange the display in a prominent position where other children and visitors can see it, such as a foyer or the school hall.

Photocopiable

HISTORY

When do we have holidays?

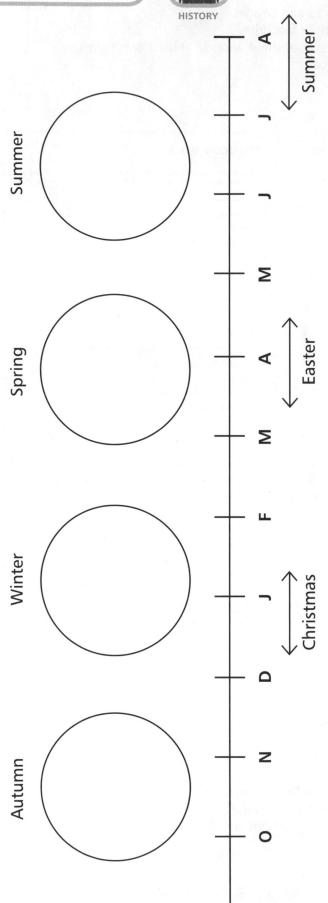

Autumn — Winter — Spring — Summer

S — O — N — D — J — F — M — A — M — J — J — A

Christmas

Easter

Summer

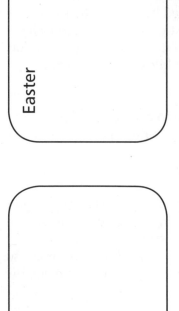

Christmas

Easter

Summer

In which season is your birthday? _____

What is the nearest holiday to your birthday? _____

SCHOLASTIC

16

GEOGRAPHY

Holiday places

town

countryside

seaside

 GEOGRAPHY

Using a map

Key:

	towns		countryside		seaside places

■ SCHOLASTIC

Going to the seaside

FOCUS

GEOGRAPHY

GEOGRAPHY
- experiences of the seaside
- familiar seaside places
- physical features of seaside places
- effect of the weather at the seaside
- mapwork

HISTORY

HISTORY
- recalling and sharing personal experiences
- features associated with seaside holidays

Preparation for section 2

Be prepared to include any children who might not have visited the seaside, for example by allowing them to talk about stories or television programmes set at the seaside.

GEOGRAPHY   HISTORY

ACTIVITY 1

WE DO LIKE TO BE BESIDE THE SEASIDE

Learning objectives
To recall personal experiences of the seaside; to investigate places.

Resources
Pictures, books, poems and stories relating to events and experiences at the seaside; paper; pencils and crayons.

Activity
Show the children a picture of a typical seaside scene and read a story or poem. Encourage the children to share their experiences, perhaps in turn or in answer to questions. Ask what the seaside is like. What is it that attracts people to have a holiday there? What things do children enjoy the most? What do they look forward to before they go? What was the weather like when they were last by the sea? Was the seaside place in this country or abroad?

Organise the children into pairs and suggest they take turns to tell each other about their seaside experiences and incidents they recall. Suggest they tell each other how they travelled there and which things they liked most about the seaside. Let them compare the details of the places they visited.

Allow about five minutes for the conversations and then ask the children if they have found out anything that was the same about both places. Have any children found unexpected differences? Perhaps one place had a harbour with boats, another just a sandy beach.

Recording
Ask the children to draw and write about their personal experiences of the seaside. Some children could directly compare their own experiences with that of their partner. Perhaps encourage the children to write as if sending a postcard to a friend.

Differentiation
Children:
■ talk about their seaside experiences and record with drawings and simple sentences
■ share experiences of the seaside; make and record comparisons between different places
■ take part in a discussion about the seaside, recording their experiences, and making useful comparisons.

Plenary
Point out that people's experiences of the seaside are usually enjoyable. If appropriate, point out that many people like to visit seaside places because they are so different from their own locality.

Display
Arrange the children's personal accounts with the pictures and books and any poems.

GEOGRAPHY   HISTORY

ACTIVITY 2

OUR NEAREST SEASIDE PLACE

Learning objective
To use maps and atlases to find familiar places.

Resources
A large map of the British Isles (see section 1, activity 4); atlases; large scale local maps; photocopiable page 18; pencils and crayons; board or flip chart.

Preparation
Mark the children's village or town on the map. You will need to consider other seaside places if the children live at the seaside. Adapt photocopiable page 18 by providing a new title, 'Our nearest seaside place', and adding sentences at the bottom of the page for the children to complete: *Our nearest seaside place is ___ ; I would travel there by ___ .*

Activity
Ask the children where the nearest seaside place is to their home. Write suggestions on the board. Discuss how you would travel to these places. Perhaps it is possible to walk down to the beach. Maybe a short car or bus journey will get you there. If the seaside is further away, you will need to go by car, coach or train.

Display a large map of the British Isles. Ask the children to remind each other which part of the map represents the land and which the sea. Choose a child to demonstrate where the main coastline is by tracing it with a finger. Comment that, as there is a lot of coastline, there must be many places by the sea. Some countries do not have so much coastline and others have none at all. (Show Austria, for example, on a map of Europe in one of the atlases.)

Point out the sticker marking the place where the children live. Ask volunteers to trace a line from the sticker to the sea. Do this in several directions as appropriate. Ask the children which seems to be the shortest route. Point out that people would not be able to travel in such a straight line because the roads/railway tracks have to make their way through the countryside.

Give atlases to pairs of children. Tell them to study the map of Britain to find the nearest point on the coastline to their home, as well as to other places they know (such as their grandparents' town). Show how the places are represented by dots, with the name close by.

After a few minutes, bring the children together and find out if they have found familiar places. Are they seaside places they have visited? Could they easily match dots with names? Do the children agree on which is the nearest seaside place to where they live? On the large map, demonstrate how to mark the place accurately and label it.

Mention that many children will live at this seaside place, so their home is by the sea. They might be able just to walk down to the beach. Make generalisations about how near to the sea the children live: *We live in the middle of the country so we are a long way from the seaside; We can reach the sea in two directions; It takes us about an hour in the car to reach the sea; Lots of people have visited Skegness because you can get there and back in a day.*

Recording
Provide the children with photocopiable page 18 and ask them to put in the seaside place(s) nearest to their home. Suggest they use the map in the atlas to help them, or refer to the class map. Point out the sentences to complete. Some children could perhaps make a small drawing to represent the method they would choose to travel to this seaside place.

Differentiation
Children:
■ with help, use a simple map to find familiar places and mark them on a map of their own
■ begin to know how to use a map, find familiar places and mark them on their own map
■ confidently use a map to find familiar places and mark them on a map of their own

Plenary
Establish the seaside place you would go to if you wanted to make a short trip to the coast. Point out how helpful it is to use a map to find out where different places are.

Display
Continue to develop the map display begun in section 1. Print out the general statements relating to the nearest seaside place and arrange them near the large map. Mark further seaside places on the large map.

GEOGRAPHY   HISTORY

ACTIVITY 3

WHAT IS IT LIKE AT THE SEASIDE?

Learning objective
To be aware of some of the physical features characteristic of a seaside place.

Resources
Photographs, postcards, books and video film clearly showing physical features of seaside places; key word cards (see Preparation); photocopiable page 25; pencils and crayons.

Preparation
When finding images and a story about the physical features of the seaside, try to avoid human images, which are discussed in the following activity. Make vocabulary cards to include words such as *sea, sand, land, pebbles, beach, waves, grains, tide, shells, rocks, rock pools, dunes, cliffs;* and adjectives such as *wet, dry, damp, steep, soft, smooth, tiny, steep, alive, round, sandy, high, low, sharp, rough, yellow, blue, grey, warm, cold, pretty, patterned.*

2

Going to
the seaside

Activity
Show a short video film and a series of pictures and perhaps read a picture story book to introduce this aspect of the topic. Then ask the children to identify typical seaside features they recognise. If you have a large picture, use Blu-Tack to attach labels to the picture as the features are identified and discussed. Make sure the children understand that the seaside is where the land meets the sea. Explain that the land can be rocky or sandy, perhaps with cliffs or dunes. The beach can be sandy or pebbly. Sand grains are very small and pebbles are rounded and smoothed by the sea. The sea has waves and moves up and down the beach twice each day as tides. Shells are often found on the beach and small creatures can be seen in rock pools.

Remind the children of their nearest seaside place and decide which features can be seen there. Perhaps the place has a sandy beach and dunes but neither cliffs nor rock pools. Have any of the children visited a place that has these other features? Which features does every seaside place have?

Produce the adjectives cards. Ask the children to read one at a time and consider which feature it could describe. Some adjectives will describe several features.

Recording
Show the children photocopiable page 25. Point out where they can draw a picture of the seaside showing as many of the features as they can. Read the lists of nouns and adjectives with the children, adding any that have come up during discussion. Ask the children to use some of these in writing appropriate phrases to describe their illustration. For example they could draw a *sandy beach* with some *smooth pebbles* and *patterned shells*. There might be a *low tide* and a *blue sea*.

Differentiation
Children:
■ identify some physical features found at the seaside and show them in a drawing
■ identify and describe physical features found at the seaside, showing them in a drawing and writing descriptions
■ understand that there are features characteristic of seaside places, describe these and show them in a drawing.

Plenary
Ask the children to recall the physical features particular to the seaside. Suggest they provide an adjective to describe each feature they name.

Display
Create a large seaside landscape together. Use paints and collage materials, perhaps developing a 3-D effect with pebbles and driftwood. Use labels to identify physical features.

GEOGRAPHY HISTORY

ACTIVITY 4

WE LIKE THE SEASIDE

Learning objectives
To identify and discuss features associated with seaside holidays; to encourage speaking and listening about seaside experiences.

Resources
Paper and pencils.

Activity

Tell the children that people who live inland have always liked going to the seaside because it was usually different from where they normally lived. They enjoyed the sea, sand, fresh air and the special scenery you get on the coast. People also wanted to do other things while they were there, so particular amusements and entertainments developed. Ask the children to close their eyes for a minute and think of all the different things they look forward to when visiting the seaside. Choose some children to talk about enjoyable experiences, which might be building sandcastles, paddling in the sea, enjoying a boat trip and so on. Develop the discussion by emphasising the children's opinions of *why* they like the seaside, rather than just descriptions they give of their past holidays. Talk about special experiences to be enjoyed that cannot be found in the locality where they live. Ask the children to listen to each other so they can endorse an idea or offer alternative suggestions. Point out that by listening carefully they will not repeat what has been said and can perhaps move on to something new.

Move on to other features the children know they will find at the seaside, such as amusement arcades, funfairs, shops and cafés. Help the children to distinguish between experiences directly related to being by the sea and those that might take place anywhere.

Tell the children when it is time to draw the discussion to a close. Explain that everyone needs to know what has been decided; it is important to have a clear idea about what has been said and the conclusions reached. Encourage some children to summarise the ideas. Try to establish which activities the children feel are most representative of a visit to the seaside.

Recording

Depending how the discussion developed, ask the children to write about the experiences of the class when at the seaside. Some children will be able to distinguish between exclusively seaside experiences and other activities. Ask the children to write a concluding sentence to summarise the ideas expressed.

Differentiation

Children:
■ offer suggestions about why they like the seaside and listen to others during a discussion
■ identify and discuss seaside activities, offer relevant information and understand that a summary is useful
■ discuss seaside activities, distinguishing them from others, make relevant points, listen to others' ideas and provide a satisfactory summary.

Plenary

Point out how useful the discussion was for discovering other people's ideas about the seaside. Emphasise the importance of listening as well as speaking and that at the end of the discussion they were able to come to a conclusion about the activities enjoyed at the seaside.

ACTIVITY 5

GEOGRAPHY

WHAT SORT OF WEATHER DO WE LIKE AT THE SEASIDE?

Learning objective

To be aware of the effects of weather on people in relation to their surroundings.

Resources

Board or flip chart; paper; pencils and crayons.

2

Going to the seaside

Activity

Start by discussing the weather. *What is it like outside today? Is it wet or dry? Cold, warm or really hot? Very windy, breezy or quite calm? Will playtime be enjoyable in this weather? Will you need your coats on? Are there clouds covering the sun and making the air feel chilly?* Perhaps it will be too wet to go out. Ask the children if weather like today's would be good weather for being at the seaside. If they think so, talk about the things they would be able to do. Is it warm enough to feel comfortable in holiday clothes and swimwear? Could they play on the beach happily? If it is windy, talk about the sand blowing everywhere and how difficult it can be walking near the sea in strong winds. Talk about wet weather and how unpleasant it can be when you want to be outside. What would the children be prevented from doing if it was raining hard when they were at the seaside?

Ask the children to describe the ideal weather for the seaside and to tell you why. Note the conditions and activities suggested. Sun will be at the top of the list, as it is important for enjoying the beach and the sea. Do the children feel happier when the sun is shining? Make sure they are also aware of the dangers of the sun and measures to prevent sunburn. Tell them they should always use sunscreen and wear hats.

Ask the children how they feel when it is windy. Do they enjoy the sensation of wind blowing their hair? Ask which holiday activities need a certain amount of wind, such as flying kites and sailing boats. Discuss the implications of stormy weather by the sea, that walking on cliffs or harbour walls is dangerous, and being out in a small boat is hazardous.

Talk about what happens when it rains on holiday. Describe having to put on rainwear and how difficult it can be to enjoy yourself with lots of extra clothes on and water dripping everywhere. Are there special activities provided at seaside places to keep people amused when it is raining?

Conclude that the weather plays an important part in enjoying a holiday at the seaside.

Recording

Ask the children to draw and caption two scenes: 'A hot, sunny day at the seaside' and 'A rainy day at the seaside'. In one picture the weather is ideal and the children can show people enjoying a holiday. The contrasting picture should show the effects of rain on holidaymakers. If appropriate, discuss how the children can depict themselves in these two situations.

Differentiation

Children:
■ are aware of the effects of weather on people at the seaside, recording with illustrations
■ make links between weather conditions and the activities of people on holiday, showing comparisons when recording
■ understand some of the effects the weather can have on people, particularly those on holiday at the seaside, indicating these when recording.

Plenary

Emphasise the link between the weather and the outdoor activities of people, particularly those on holiday. Mention that many people like to visit other countries for some holidays because they know it will be warmer and sunnier than in this country. Point out that people in this country are often talking about the weather and usually ask people what the weather was like while they were on holiday. This is because the weather plays an important part in determining what we do.

Display

Mount the children's drawings and create weather effects to enhance the display.

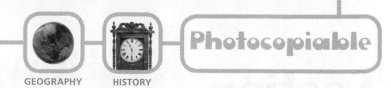

GEOGRAPHY   HISTORY

Photocopiable

What is it like at the seaside?

adjectives	
patterned	high
rocky	smooth
sandy	blue
pebbly	
low	

nouns	
beach	sea
sand	shells
cliff	pool
dunes	grains
waves	pebbles

■SCHOLASTIC

Section 3

How is the seaside different from our locality?

FOCUS

GEOGRAPHY

- differences between the local area and a seaside place
- looking at uses of land in two areas
- different buildings
- mapwork

GEOGRAPHY

ACTIVITY 1

GEOGRAPHY

USING AERIAL PHOTOGRAPHS

Learning objective

To recognise prominent features of a locality from aerial photographs.

Resources

Large aerial photographs of the children's locality and of a seaside place (several copies of each would be ideal so that the children can study them in groups); magnifying aids; board or flip chart; paper; pencils and crayons.

© Ikon Imaging

Preparation

Decide on the organisation of the activity so that all children will be able to look closely at the aerial photographs. If there are several copies of each photograph, the children can work simultaneously, otherwise the groups will need to work in turn.

Activity

Tell the children that the best view of any large part of the Earth is from a plane or satellite. Looking down, you can see all the features together that you cannot see when on the ground because of obstructions. However, the view will be different because everything is seen from above. Show the children an aerial photograph of their local area. Elicit their initial comments. What are the features that stand out? Perhaps the area is mainly green, or perhaps buildings fill the photograph? There might be a river, motorway or railway snaking across the scene. Can the children distinguish between buildings and open spaces? Are there any familiar buildings that can be identified, such as a church, football stadium or castle? Talk about how different the buildings look from above. Can the children find their own street or even their own house? Encourage the use of magnifying aids. Build up a list of words and phrases that create a picture of the area. These could include *many houses, rows of streets, church tower, lots of trees, playing field, winding river, motorway, bridges, a quarry*.

Next, show the children the aerial photograph of a seaside place. How can they tell the place is by the sea? Discuss how easy it is to distinguish between sea and land. Trace the coastline to emphasise the point where the land meets the sea. Ask the children to compare the area of land with that of the sea. They will notice how the land is crowded with buildings and structures, while the area of the sea is mainly clear. Contrast the colours of land and sea if possible. Ask the children to look for features close to the sea's edge. Can they see a beach? Are there cliffs? Perhaps there is a harbour and boats are visible? Are any buildings close to the water's edge – a lifeboat house, a few rows of houses, a caravan site?

Make a list of the features on the seaside photograph that are not to be seen on the photograph of your local area. Is it a long list? Did the children think there would be so many differences? Then look for things that are similar on each photograph. Make a second list, which might include streets, houses, green areas.

Recording

Provide each child with a sheet of paper divided into two columns, headed *Our locality* and *The seaside*. Ask them to make two lists, drawing and labelling features as they observed them on the aerial photographs of their own locality and the seaside place. Refer them to the lists made during the discussion for help with spellings.

Differentiation

Children:
■ are aware of differences between a seaside place and the local area on aerial photographs
■ recognise some differences on aerial photographs between a seaside area and their own locality
■ can examine aerial photographs to make relevant comparisons between a seaside place and the local area.

Plenary

Ask the children, if they were in a plane or helicopter, how they would know whether they were flying over a seaside place or their own locality. Refer to the main features and some of the distinctive landmarks.

Display

Label the aerial photographs, highlighting similarities and differences between the two areas. These could be added to the map display.

ACTIVITY 2

A MAP OF THE SEASIDE

GEOGRAPHY

Learning objectives

To understand how simple maps can represent prominent features of a locality; to use a key.

Resources

A large map to represent an area of coast; a local map with a key; photocopiable page 34; pencils and crayons.

Preparation

To make the large map that represents part of the coast, you could use a simple enlargement

3

How is the seaside different from our locality?

of the aerial photograph used in the previous activity, or an enlargement of photocopiable page 34. Include symbols to represent some prominent features, such as cliffs, a pier or jetty, some buildings, a funfair.

Activity

Show the children the map of a seaside place. Explain that it is a representation of what would be seen on an aerial photograph. The main features have been indicated as symbols. Point out that the drawing is really a map and shows only some of the things that would be seen on an aerial photograph.

Ask the children what they can tell you about the place shown. First of all, is it a seaside place? How can they tell? Which part is the sea and which is the land? What clues did they use to help them identify sea and land? Can they tell what the coastline is like? Which part has cliffs? Is there a sandy beach? Is there a safe place for boats? Is it used as a harbour? Emphasise the natural (physical) features shown by the map: sea, land, beach, cliffs, the safe place for boats, the river.

Move on to look at the human features. Ask the children to identify any buildings or other man-made structures. They might recognise streets with buildings that could be shops or hotels, the pier, the funfair, the lifeboat house.

Tell the children that it is important to identify the features a map shows, so people using the map will know what can be found at this place. Point out that it might be possible to write in the names on the map, but it could become crowded with words and therefore unclear, so it is simpler to make a *key*, which explains the symbols in a space at the edge of the map. Explain that the symbols on the map itself must look exactly like those in the key so people reading the map will find them easily. Demonstrate how to use the key on a simple local map, perhaps one that shows the location of a leisure centre or a walking route.

Recording

Provide the children with photocopiable page 34. Show them where the key will be and ask them to compile the key by copying the symbols used to represent the features and writing their names. If appropriate, distinguish between natural and human features. Encourage the children to add colour to the map, which should also be used appropriately in the key. Ask the children to suggest colours to use – perhaps blue for the sea and river, yellow for sand, brown for rocks and cliffs. Some children might like to add extra features to their maps.

Differentiation

Children:
■ begin to understand the use of symbols on a map and with help complete a key
■ know that symbols can represent features on a map and that a key is important; complete a simple key
■ understand that symbols and a key are important when representing features on a map; provide a key.

Plenary

Ask the children why a key is important when reading a map. Look at some of the children's maps and check if the symbols on the map are the same as those in the key. Point out that a map of a different place might require some different symbols, as there could be other features to show.

Display

Add the large maps and the children's work to develop the map display.

ACTIVITY 3

WHERE WE LIVE

GEOGRAPHY

Learning objective
To review the use of land and buildings in the immediate locality.

Resources
Aerial photographs of the locality; photocopiable page 35; pencils and crayons.

Preparation
It will be helpful if the children are aware of the concept of land use and have experienced through fieldwork and mapwork the uses of land and buildings in their locality. Before photocopying page 35, add any words or phrases to the vocabulary section that specifically relate to important uses of land in the local area as identified on the aerial photograph.

Activity
Refer to the aerial photographs the children have seen of their locality (activity 1). Help the children to become aware of the nature of their surroundings in three stages:
■ First, encourage them to describe an overall picture of the area as determined by the colour. It might be mostly green, with fields, woods and trees and only small clusters of buildings. It might be a built up area, with streets and blocks of buildings covering the photograph, in which case the main colour might appear brown or grey with a striped and speckled effect.
■ Next, identify continuous features, such as a river or motorway, and any prominent landmarks, such as a tower, stadium or castle. There might be obvious industrial development.
■ Finally, describe details such as streets, other buildings, and small pockets of open space. Talk to the children about how the land is used in their part of the world. Did they realise it was so green/so crowded with buildings? Consider whether the impression we get on the ground matches the reality shown by the photographs. Did the children realise there were so many trees? That the golf course or factory took up so much space? That the path of the river or the motorway is so winding? That the streets make a pattern?
  By studying the photographs and using the children's experience of the area, help them to decide what the main uses of the land in their neighbourhood are. Organise their suggestions into three groups to represent the uses of most of the land, some of the land and only a little of the land. For example, *most of the land is covered by fields and trees; some of the land is covered by streets and houses; a little of the land is covered by a railway and a factory*. As the discussion develops, refer to examples with which the children are familiar as they travel around their neighbourhood. Talk about the types of buildings to be found in the area. Are they mostly houses? Are there any industrial buildings? Are there buildings connected with farming activities?

Recording
Show the children photocopiable page 35 and read the words describing the uses of land. Ask the children to write these words in the appropriate boxes according to whether the features and buildings cover most of the land in the local area, some of the land, or a little of the land. They can add illustrations or symbols as appropriate.

Differentiation
Children:
■ with help, identify some uses of land in the local area, recognising some of the main features

■ identify different uses of land in the local area, recording their frequency
■ identify and begin to understand the different uses of land in the local area, recording their frequency.

Plenary
Remind the children of the main uses of land in their area and ask them to tell you what type most of the buildings are.

Display
Use work from this activity to enhance the map display.

ACTIVITY 4

GEOGRAPHY

LOOKING FOR DIFFERENCES

Learning objective
To compare land use in the immediate locality with that in a seaside area.

Resources
Aerial photographs of a seaside area and the local area (see activity 1); illustrations and photographs of different coastlines and activities that take place at the seaside; board or flip chart; paper; pencils and crayons.

Activity
Look again at the aerial photograph of the seaside place. Ask the children if they notice any immediate differences between it and the photograph of their local area from the previous activity. They should easily recognise the coastline. Do they think the land part looks similar to that of their local area? Perhaps both areas are mostly green or both are covered with buildings. Perhaps they look very different at a glance.

Encourage the children to look closely at the coastline. What can they find out about the land where it meets the sea? Can they tell what is it used for? Is there a big or small area of sand? Can any sand dunes or cliffs be identified? Is there a harbour? Are there footpaths or roads to be seen? Show the children pictures of typical coastal landscapes and relate these to what they have recognised from the aerial photographs.

Perhaps the children can make out buildings. Do they look like houses? Are there holiday chalets and caravans? Can they see a pattern of streets?

Look at the open spaces on the photograph and decide what the land is used for there. There might be a golf course, boating lake, a park with gardens, a funfair. Can the children see paths where people might walk?

Ask the children to think of any activities they might take part in if they were on holiday at this seaside place. List these on the board. This could include playing in the sand; enjoying a trip on the boating lake; visiting the funfair; walking along the beach, through the park, to the top of the cliffs; watching the boats in the harbour. Point out how the land is used for people to enjoy themselves. Ask the children to think of other things they can do at the seaside, perhaps at different places by the sea. Show pictures to help children who might not be familiar with some of the activities.

Read through the list and decide which of the activities are available in the local area, and which are only possible at this seaside place. Use different coloured pens to distinguish between them. Perhaps there are activities the children can take part in locally that are not possible at the seaside.

Recording

Provide the children with sheets of paper divided into two and ask them to draw and caption one or more activities they would be able to enjoy only at the seaside, and those they can enjoy in their own locality. Headings could be 'What I can do at the seaside' and 'What I can do here'. Some children can write sentences to make comparisons.

Differentiation

Children:
■ recognise and describe through drawings some differences between the uses of land in their own locality and those in a seaside environment
■ recognise some differences between the uses of land in their own locality and in a seaside environment; describe these using drawings and sentences
■ recognise a range of differences between land use in their own locality and in a seaside environment, describing and making comparisons through drawings and sentences.

Plenary

Remind the children that the land is likely to be very different at the seaside from their own locality. People use the land in different ways. Help the children to appreciate that at the seaside, the land is often used to provide activities for people who are on holiday and have time to enjoy themselves.

Display

Work on the local area can be displayed to contrast with a seaside location if appropriate.

ACTIVITY 5

DIFFERENT BUILDINGS

GEOGRAPHY

Learning objective

To be aware of some differences between buildings in the locality and those at the seaside.

Resources

Aerial photographs; photographs, postcards and stories relating to buildings associated with the locality and those associated with the seaside.

Preparation

It is helpful if the children have looked at the range of buildings in their locality.

Activity

Start by asking the children to tell you as many different buildings in their neighbourhood
as they can. Then ask the children what buildings and structures they might expect to see
at the seaside. Refer to any identified buildings on the aerial photographs and use pictures
so that all the children can relate to what is being discussed. Include other buildings specific
to seaside areas that were not apparent on the aerial photograph, but might be within
some of the children's experiences. Explain, for example, that a pier was constructed so that
people could enjoy a walk out over the sea and that a jetty is where boats can be tied up.
A lighthouse or beacon is important to warn ships where there are dangerous rocks in the
area. Talk about buildings constructed with the special purpose of amusing and entertaining
holidaymakers: perhaps a theatre; a
funfair; a games arcade; kiosks for
selling toys, ice cream, tickets.

Look at the arrangement of roads
and houses on the aerial photograph;
point out that people like to have a
view of the sea and that hotels and
guest houses usually face the sea.
Perhaps the children have had caravan
holidays by the sea and know that
most seaside places have caravan
parks with associated buildings.

Ask the children to help you make
a list of the buildings and structures
that are found at the seaside but
not in their own locality. This might
include a pier, a harbour, a lighthouse,
beach huts, a lifeboat station, hotels,
amusement arcades, ice cream kiosks
and souvenir shops.

Can the children suggest any reasons
why there are differences in the uses of buildings in their locality and at a seaside place? Do
more people visit the seaside than their own area?

Recording

Ask the children to draw and name six different seaside buildings: three that are found at
the seaside and three that relate especially to people on holiday. On the reverse of the page,
some children can write sentences to explain why these buildings are found at the seaside,
and not in their local area.

Differentiation

Children:
■ recognise, draw and label some buildings that are found at the seaside
■ can identify and describe different buildings found at the seaside, providing some reasons
as to why they are specific to coastal places
■ can identify, describe and give reasons why different buildings are found at the seaside,
making comparisons with buildings in their own locality.

Plenary

Ask the children why there is not a lighthouse or beach hut in their locality. Why are they only
built by the sea? What do the children think is the biggest difference between the use of the
buildings where they live and those at a seaside place?

Display

Make a frieze of typical seaside buildings using photographs and the children's drawings.

ACTIVITY 6

IF I LIVED BY THE SEA

GEOGRAPHY

Learning objective
To be aware of differences between living in the children's own area and living by the sea.

Resources
The children's work and accumulated resources from the previous activities; seaside brochures and guidebooks; board or flip chart; paper; pencils.

Preparation
Read a story to the children that describes living by the sea.

Activity
Ask the children if they would like to live by the sea. Encourage them to share the reasons for their choices. There might be children who have moved to the local area from a seaside place who can describe what it is like to live by the sea.

Suggest that the children talk to each other in pairs about what they would do if they lived at the seaside that they are unable to do in the place they live now. Give them about five minutes, and let them use the brochures and guidebooks for ideas. Then make two lists to compare activities the children can do in the local area and those they would be able to do if they lived by the sea.

Consider the children's suggestions and make comparisons relating to a range of activities. For instance, where would parents/carers take children to play? What might they do for a birthday treat? Where would they go for a walk? Where would they go for a picnic or to look at the view? What might they see from their bedroom window? What could they do on a rainy day? Compare the lifestyle at home with living by the sea.

Recording
Ask the children to write about living at the seaside, explaining what they would be able to do each day. If appropriate, provide a sequence of prompts relating to the areas discussed to help them cover a range of ideas. As a conclusion, they can decide whether they would prefer life at the seaside to living where they do.

Differentiation
Children:
■ describe what they think it would be like to live at the seaside using simple sentences
■ write a description of life at the seaside, making some comparisons with their local area
■ write a detailed description of life at the seaside, making comparisons with living in their own locality, and discussing where they would prefer to be.

Plenary
Talk about how everyone likes to visit the seaside because there are different things to do, and that some people actually live there. Point out that people who live by the sea probably like to visit other areas for their holidays – cities and countryside inland as well as other seaside places – so they can have different experiences. Perhaps seaside dwellers would find the children's locality an interesting place for a holiday.

GEOGRAPHY

A map of the seaside

Key:

	river				

CURRICULUM LINKS ages 5–7: The seaside

GEOGRAPHY

Where we live

a little of the land

some of the land

most of the land

golf course

lake

roads

trees

woods

factories

park

houses

farms

river

motorway

What was the seaside like in the past?

FOCUS

HISTORY

HISTORY
■ using a range of resources to find out about the past
■ discovering information from pictures, photographs and artefacts
■ asking questions
■ identifying changes

GEOGRAPHY

GEOGRAPHY
■ comparing features of the seaside today with those of the past
■ using and presenting geographical information

HISTORY

ACTIVITY 1

LOOKING FOR CLUES

Learning objectives
To sequence photographs into three time periods by identifying differences between present and past; to use a variety of resources to find out information.

Resources
A collection of photographs and postcards depicting seaside holiday activities from three different periods in time: present day, parents' era, grandparents' era; photocopiable page 44; board or flip chart; pencils and crayons.

Preparation
Find photographs from three periods (grandparents', parents' and the present) that show contrasts in clothing, hairstyles and seaside activities and perhaps include buildings, vehicles and advertising signs. If using several photographs from each era to show a range of features, mount these on three large pieces of card to represent each period of time. A few days before the activity, ask the children to talk to their parents/carers and grandparents about seaside holidays when they were young. Suggest the children remember one especially interesting snippet of information from their parents and one from their grandparents.

Activity
Show the children the three sets of photographs and if it is not immediately obvious, tell them that the pictures were all taken at the seaside. Ask if they notice anything different about the three groups. They might suggest that some pictures seem old fashioned while one group looks very familiar. Explain that the groups represent different times at the seaside: one is modern and the other two are from times in the past.

Ask the children to help you put the pictures in chronological order. Ask the children how they can tell which photographs were taken fairly recently. They might recognise children like themselves. They will be familiar with styles of dress, toys and modern surroundings. The photographs themselves might look new and bright. Then ask the children to distinguish between the two older sets of photographs. Are there any clues that might help?

To help with this, ask the children to share their parents' and grandparents' memories with the class. Try to group the information so that the children can begin to distinguish between the two periods of time. Perhaps make notes of some of the information, such as the accommodation people stayed in, who they went on holiday with, how they travelled about, games they played on the beach, what they did when it rained. Make two distinct lists for reference. Add to these lists the information gleaned from the old photographs.

Recording
On photocopiable page 44, draw attention to the headings that represent three periods of time. Ask the children to write words or sentences to describe what they enjoy doing at the seaside, then what they have discovered their parents and grandparents remember doing. They can add illustrations in the boxes. Some children might use a theme, for example: *I went to the seaside by car. My dad travelled to Skegness by coach. My gran went by train…*

Differentiation
Children:
■ are aware that there are differences between holidays at the seaside now and in the past, recording with drawings and simple sentences
■ begin to understand the differences between seaside holidays now and in the past, recording with drawings and sentences
■ recognise some differences between seaside holidays now and at two different periods of time in the past, recording details with sentences and drawings.

Plenary
Remind the children that they have used pictures and people's memories to discover some of the differences between seaside holidays now and in the past. Point out that things are always changing and children in the future will probably have seaside holidays that in many ways will be different from those the children enjoy today.

Display
Begin to create a display on the theme of the seaside in the past. Use the photographs and pictures with the children's work from this activity.

GEOGRAPHY

HISTORY

ACTIVITY 2

NOW AND THEN

Learning objectives
To sort information into categories that distinguish the past from the present; to use time-related vocabulary.

Resources
Photographs and postcards from the previous activity plus an additional one from grandparents' time; magnifying aids; pencils and crayons.

Preparation
Copy the photograph from the children's grandparents' time onto the centre of a recording sheet. Try to find one that shows features that the children can compare and contrast with the seaside today.

4

What was the seaside like in the past?

Activity

Remind the children how they sequenced photographs to show the seaside at different periods. Encourage them now to look more closely at the photographs to discover more features. First look at the clothing and hairstyles in the old photographs. What are the swimsuits like? What are the adults wearing? Perhaps some men are wearing suits and ties. Does this seem strange for holiday wear? What are the women's dresses like? Are they wearing hats? Are they sunhats? Are the holidaymakers carrying things such as picnic baskets or beach toys? Are the hairstyles very different from those of today? Is anyone wearing sunglasses? What were the shoes like that people wore at the seaside in the past?

  Look at the activities children in the photographs are involved in. Are they doing things children like to do today, such as making sandcastles? Decide whether seaside activities have changed or are much the same. Use vocabulary such as *recent, modern, old fashioned, oldest*.

  Where appropriate, draw attention to the setting. What is in the background that shows this is the past? What clues show the scenes are not modern? Talk about details. If there are buildings, are the signs and so on different from today? What can this tell us about the past? Are there any vehicles to be seen? Do they look old fashioned or modern?

Recording

Show the children the sheet with the old photograph. Ask the children how they can tell the picture is of a beach scene in their grandparents' time, considering clothes, hairstyles, beach facilities, transport and surroundings. Let them label features on the picture and/or write in sentences. The children could draw and describe an equivalent modern seaside scene, indicating how they have made their picture look modern.

Differentiation

Children:
■ are aware that there are different categories of information that distinguish the present from the past, indicating these using drawings and words
■ identify different categories of information to distinguish the present from the past, recording through drawing and sentences
■ identify and describe different information that distinguishes the present from the past.

Plenary

Point out to the children that they have used a variety of clues from pictures to discover more about what it was like at the seaside in the past. Ask them to remind each other of some of the categories they used, such as clothes, activities, vehicles, buildings.

Display

Include a section of the display where comparisons can be made with the seaside today.

HISTORY

ACTIVITY 3

ASKING QUESTIONS

Learning objective

To find out about seaside holidays in the past by asking questions of an adult visitor.

Resources

A visitor who can speak to the children, show artefacts and souvenirs and answer their questions about seaside holidays in the past; additional seaside artefacts; board or flip chart; still or video camera; paper; pencils.

Preparation

Discuss with the visitor how the activity will proceed. Find out what experiences he or she can share with the children. If necessary, borrow additional artefacts and souvenirs from the school collection, local museum or parents. Suggest the visitor speaks for a short time, perhaps with anecdotes of his/her memories of seaside holidays as a child, before the children ask questions they have prepared. If appropriate, provide the visitor with a list of the questions beforehand. Ask permission if you would like to take photographs or video of the talk. Arrange furniture for comfort and to display the artefacts.

Activity

Explain to the children that someone will be visiting the class who remembers what it was like to go to the seaside many years ago. This person will talk about his/her holidays and answer questions the children would like to ask. Tell them who the visitor is and whether his childhood corresponds with the children's parents or grandparents.

Ask the children to think about what they would like to know about the seaside from someone who enjoyed holidays there when they were young. Emphasise that this person remembers what happened a long time ago when he was a child and that the information the children will find out is first-hand.

Ask the children to suggest questions to put to the visitor. Write them on the board. Then get the children to look at the questions again to edit them. Decide if some questions are nearly the same and can be removed or combined. Can the questions be grouped and put in a logical order? Plan who is to ask the individual questions. Perhaps allow rehearsal time.

Tell the children when the visitor is expected, how he should be greeted, how they are expected to behave, when they should listen and when there is an opportunity to ask their questions. Emphasise how important it will be to say thank you to the visitor who is giving his/her time and helping them to find out about the past.

On the day of the visit briefly remind the children of their responsibilities. Introduce the visitor and be prepared to take photographs when appropriate.

Lead the question session, inviting the children to speak in turn: *I think George and Sarah have the next question.* Prompt where necessary, otherwise allow the children to speak independently. Ask a question yourself towards the end to cover interesting aspects that have arisen during the talk.

Ensure the children show their appreciation for the time and expertise given by the visitor.

Recording

Ask the children to write out the question they asked and perhaps one asked by a friend, and to record what they found out from the replies. Some children might be able to make comments about the information discovered.

Differentiation

Children:
■ are aware that they can find out information about the past by asking questions
■ understand that they can find out about the past by asking questions, reporting the information discovered
■ begin to understand the significance of asking relevant questions to find out about the past, reporting in detail the information discovered.

Plenary

Remind the children how useful it is to be able to ask questions of experts to find out about what happened in the past. Emphasise the valuable help provided by the visitor. Discuss some of the surprising information they found out.

Display

Arrange any artefacts and photographs where they can be seen by the children during this and later work.

What was the seaside like in the past?

ACTIVITY 4

SOUVENIRS

What was the seaside like in the past?

Learning objective
To select relevant information about seaside holidays in the past.

Resources
A selection of souvenirs brought back from seaside holidays in the past; paper; pencils and crayons.

Preparation
Collect appropriate seaside souvenirs from the class collection and those loaned by parents and the museum service. Try to include a train, bus, boat or tram ticket; theatre ticket or programme; an old toy that might have been taken on the trip; postcards; advertising material, leaflets and guide books; an ornament or trinket labelled *A gift from...* or in the shape of some local landmark such as a lighthouse or tower. Also include items from a beach, such as interesting driftwood, shells, pebbles, or even fossils.

Activity
Display the souvenirs and elicit the children's comments. Have they seen things like these before? Where? Notice that they have all been brought back from seaside holidays. Identify the items. Read any place names or other written information, and focus on any images. Ask the children if any of the items look really old. Perhaps those made of paper are tattered and torn; others might be chipped, scratched or faded. Some things might be in very good condition but are old-fashioned. Ask the children why people have always liked to bring things back from their holidays. Talk about wanting to be reminded of an interesting place, remembering a happy time, buying presents for people. Tell the children that such objects are called souvenirs. Try to explain that in the past, there was not such a range of things to buy as there is today and so gifts bought at the seaside were precious and treasured for a long time. Ask the children if they have collections of similar treasures at home.

Ask the children what clues they can spot among the souvenirs that tell them about seaside holidays in the past. Perhaps some objects have pictures that show what a place used to be like. Highlight details on theatre programmes, tickets and advertising material that are different from modern equivalents. If appropriate, talk about the materials from which the ornaments and toys are made. Ask which items do not give clues about holidays in the past. The children will recognise that shells and pebbles do not tell us about the past in the same way. Although they might have been brought back as souvenirs from holidays in the past, they probably look the same as if they were collected only recently.

Recording
Ask the children to draw some of the souvenirs they examined. Explain that as the objects tell us important details about the past, the drawings should be accurate. Suggest they add captions to identify each object and record the information it gives about a seaside holiday.

Differentiation
Children:
■ recognise a souvenir and are aware that it can tell them about holidays in the past

- recognise different souvenirs and identify clues about holidays in the past
- recognise souvenirs; understand and describe how they can provide information about holidays in the past.

Plenary
Ask the children to remind each other what a souvenir is and how it can provide information. Encourage the children to talk about their own souvenirs and speculate on what information they might give future historians.

Display
Arrange the souvenirs with the children's drawings. Suggest that the children each bring a souvenir of a recent holiday they enjoyed to make a collection of modern souvenirs.

ACTIVITY 5

CHANGES

HISTORY

Learning objective
To recognise that some things change and others stay the same.

Resources
A collection of pictures, postcards and photographs showing seaside holidays of today as well as those of the past; photocopiable page 45; board or flip chart; pencils and crayons.

Preparation
Select suitable images that contrast modern seaside places and activities with those of the past. If possible, include photographs of the same place in different eras, and different generations of the same family on holiday.

Activity
Ask the children to recall what they have discovered about seaside holidays in the past. Point out that many things have changed but others are still the same. Children in the past probably enjoyed seaside holidays in much the same way as children today. Refer to the visitor the children were able to talk to during activity 3, and their parents and grandparents, and suggest there are things they enjoyed at the seaside that children of today also enjoy. Encourage the children to help you make a list of these things that have not changed, for example making sandcastles, playing ball games, having a picnic, paddling, looking for crabs, collecting pebbles. Highlight this by showing comparable photographs of children in the past enjoying similar activities to children today.

Make a second list of things that *have* changed. Do they take part in any seaside activities that children of the past would not have known about, such as playing with modern toys, arcade games or new fairground rides?

Using photographs, ask the children whether a particular seaside holiday place has changed. Perhaps buildings and features look similar but have new signs, or lots of cars parked outside, or different uses. What do the children think are new additions to a holiday resort? Explain that large theme parks and computer-game arcades are modern attractions that their grandparents and perhaps parents would not have experienced.

Recording
Show the children the illustrations on photocopiable page 45. Explain that one picture shows children at the seaside in the past and the second picture children of today at the seaside.

Ask them to write about the things that are the same in each picture and the things that are different.

Differentiation
Children:
■ recognise that some things stay the same and others change, recording this simply with words and phrases
■ identify some things that have stayed the same and others that have changed, recording with relevant notes
■ identify things that have stayed the same and those that have changed, recording in detail.

Plenary
Reinforce the children's understanding that although there are always changes at a place, some things do stay the same. Children in the future will still enjoy activities children have always liked, some buildings will remain, landscape features may have different uses. If the children visit a place again when they are grown up, they will certainly notice some changes.

Display
Continue the 'seaside in the past' display, perhaps developing a frieze with paintings and other illustrations by the children.

GEOGRAPHY   HISTORY

ACTIVITY 6

CREATING A POSTER

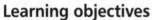

Learning objectives
To use information acquired about the past to develop a poster; to recognise features of the seaside in the past.

Resources
A collection of items relating to the seaside in the past, representing either the children's grandparents' or parents' childhood, especially postcards, posters, photographs and souvenirs of times past; board or flip chart; poster paper; different colours of drawing paper; glue; pencils and crayons.

Preparation
Decide on a seaside resort the children are familiar with and about which you have sufficient reference resources. Alternatively, invent a place around which a picture of the seaside in the past can be developed. Provide the children with suitable background paper and smaller pieces of drawing paper on which to write promotional slogans. These can be cut out as thought or speech bubbles to be glued onto the background.

Activity
Ask the children how they can pass on some of the information they have discovered about seaside holidays in the past. Suggest one way is to recreate a poster that would have been used to advertise a resort and encourage people to visit. Explain that the poster will need only a few words and should be designed to give people an impression of the seaside without a lot of reading.

Tell the children the name of the resort you have in mind, examine the photographs and artefacts and discuss which features of the place people ought to know about. Which are the most appealing? Make a list of the children's ideas – for example, the sandy beach, fairground attractions, a harbour with boats, a lighthouse or other interesting landmark, good places to walk, a light railway, guest houses and hotels, shops and cafés.

Then talk about creating slogans to encourage people to visit the place. Choose each of the features of the resort in turn and think of its main appeal. Start with the beach. What will people like to know about the sand and the sea? Is there a big stretch of sand? Are there dunes? Is there a bay? How could the sand be described? Does the beach have rock pools? Is the sea safe enough for children to paddle in? Select specific information and put it together as a statement: *The beach stretches for miles, there is plenty of good sand, the sea is shallow and sometimes calm and when the tide is out there are lots of pools.* Help the children to condense their ideas by removing unnecessary words to create a really short slogan: *Miles of golden sands with safe paddling.* Follow the same process for accommodation, special buildings, amusements and so on, reminding the children that they should be thinking about the seaside resort as it was in their grandparents' or parents' childhood.

Ask the children what else a poster might need. Consider how the name of the place could be prominently displayed and what illustrations would be suitable. Consider pictures that show how people in the past would dress and behave when on holiday. Talk about a colour scheme. Ask which colours would be most suitable to use. Which ones remind people of happy holidays, blue seas and skies and sunny days on the beach?

Recording

To help the children focus on their task, provide instructions in stages, demonstrating as necessary:

1. Choose a background piece of paper of a suitable colour.

2. Decide which attractions (about three of them) to feature on the poster. Plan a slogan for each, edit and write them out in rough and check the spelling.

3. On small pieces of drawing paper, write the place name and the slogans; cut these out with some space around the lettering.

4. Arrange the separate pieces of paper on the poster paper to achieve the best effect and then glue them on.

5. In the spaces, make appropriate drawings that refer to the slogans and show people what the seaside place was like in the past.

6. Write the name of the designer discreetly at the bottom of the poster: *Designed by Oliver Johnson.*

Differentiation

Children:

■ use information discovered about the past to design a poster relating to a seaside place

■ use information discovered about the past to design a poster, including detail relating to activities, buildings and other features

■ make imaginative use of information about the past to design a poster including accurate details relating to activities, buildings and other features.

Plenary

Exhibit the posters. Ask the children for their impressions. Are the posters interesting enough to make people want to visit the seaside? Point out details that are particularly relevant in showing what seaside holidays were like in the past.

Display

Display all the posters for a short while in the classroom so that the children can view them and comment on the design features, before moving them to a more permanent site.

Looking for clues

Myself at the seaside

_____

_____

_____

_____

_____

Parents at the seaside

_____

_____

_____

Grandparents at the seaside

_____

_____

_____

_____

HISTORY

Changes

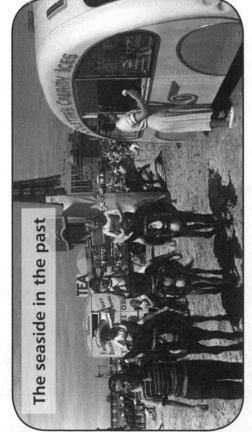

© Popperfoto/Reuters

The seaside in the past

© Getty Images/Gary Buss

The seaside today

Things that are the same:

Things that are different:

■SCHOLASTIC

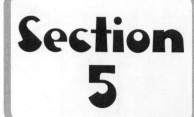

Section 5

Where else in the world...?

GEOGRAPHY

FOCUS
GEOGRAPHY
■ the wider world
■ using secondary sources
■ presenting information
■ mapwork
■ the effects of weather on holidays

GEOGRAPHY

ACTIVITY 1

SEASIDE PLACES AROUND THE WORLD

Learning objectives
To develop an awareness of the wider world; to use maps and atlases.

Resources
A globe; a large map of the world; atlases; board or flip chart; a worksheet (see Preparation); pencils.

Preparation
Prepare a worksheet that lists familiar seaside holiday destinations in other countries. If necessary, provide prompt questions to help the children with their recording: *Why do people like to visit the seaside in other countries? Which seaside places in other countries do people like to visit?*

Activity
Ask the children if any of them have been on holiday to a different country. Was it a seaside holiday? Was the weather different from in this country? Did the people speak a different language from us? Then ask the children why some people like to visit a different country for a holiday. Perhaps it is because there is more sunshine in other places and the sea is warmer. Some holidaymakers like to visit places where people speak another language, have different food and different ways of doing things. List the seaside resorts in other countries that children have visited or are familiar with.

Show the children a globe and explain that this represents the world. Identify the areas of land and ocean/sea, and Great Britain. Then locate some of the countries the children might be familiar with, for example America, France, Spain and Greece.

Next, show the children a map of the world and explain that like the globe, this also represents the world. However, because it is flat it allows us to see all the countries together. Point out Britain and ask the children to help you find countries such as America, France, Spain and Greece, then towns and cities they might have mentioned. Trace the directions travelled to reach these places and talk about the proximity to the Britain and the methods of transport required.

Provide the children with atlases and direct them to a suitable map of the world, or Europe. In pairs, give them a short list of places (some countries, some towns/cities) to find where they could have a seaside holiday. Remind them that the holiday places will be on the coast – that is, where the land meets the sea.

Recording
Provide the children with the worksheet that includes place names of seaside places abroad. Ask them to write a report on why people like to visit seaside places in other countries and which places are popular. Encourage them to include their own experiences as appropriate.

Differentiation
Children:
■ are aware that there are seaside places in other countries where people go for holidays and with help locate some of these on a map
■ know why people like to visit seaside places in other countries and locate some of the places on a map of the world
■ discuss why people like to visit seaside places in other countries, locating a range of places on a map of the world.

© Photodisc, Inc.

Plenary
Remind the children how useful maps are when locating places in other parts of the world. Ask how they know when a place on a map is by the sea.

Display
Use pins or stickers on a large world map to show holiday places around the world.

ACTIVITY 2

DIFFERENT PLACES TO VISIT

GEOGRAPHY

Learning objective
To use secondary sources to find out information.

Resources
Travel brochures; atlases; a globe; a large map of the world; scissors; glue; paper; pencils.

Activity
Show the children the travel brochures you have collected. Explain that these are provided by travel companies to show people what kind of holidays they can have in different parts of the world. Talk about an interesting holiday you have found. Tell the children where it is and what its attractions are. Suggest that you are considering going there: *I like the picture of the sandy beach with the cliffs in the background. This is the kind of scenery I like. Will I be able to go walking? I wonder if it is a busy place? Now, does the information tell me what the weather will be like in August? I hope it won't be too hot then.* Perhaps read out a description of the place so that the children can help you can check your requirements.
  In groups, ask the children to find you suitable places for a holiday. Provide them with brochures and suggest they find you a choice of holidays in several different places. If appropriate, make a list of some simple requirements on which they can focus: a sandy beach, boat trips, restaurants, warm, sunny weather. Encourage purposeful discussion and give the children ideas about how they can remember suitable places they have chosen. Perhaps they can make a simple list that includes the page number of the brochure and use removable stickers to mark relevant pages. Some children can use atlases to find the locations of the resorts that have been chosen.

Recording
When they have compiled a shortlist, ask the children to describe the places they have chosen and give their reasons. Individuals or pairs can cut out a picture of one of the seaside places, glue it to a sheet of paper and add a description. They should include in this why they think this seaside place would make a suitable holiday destination for you.

When you have read the children's reports, comment on how useful you have found the information, perhaps highlighting one or two places where you really think you might like to visit. Ask some of the children to read their reports to the rest of the class.

Differentiation
Children:
■ begin to develop an awareness of the wider world and with help collect information about different seaside places
■ develop an awareness of the wider world, collect and report information about different seaside places
■ become increasingly aware of the wider world, collecting and reporting relevant information about different seaside places.

Plenary
Refer to the seaside places in different parts of the world. Explain to the children that without actually visiting they have been able to get an idea of what places are like by looking at travel brochures.

Display
Put together the children's reports as a brochure, perhaps in a loose-leaf folder. If possible, present it as if in a travel agent's kiosk.

ACTIVITY 3

WHERE I WOULD LIKE TO GO

GEOGRAPHY

Learning objective
To present information about a distant seaside place.

Resources
Travel brochures including long-haul destinations; books and pictures about seaside places in different parts of the world; atlases; a large map of the world; board or flip chart; paper and pencils.

Activity
If the children are familiar with travel brochures, remind them of the research they did in the previous activity. Explain how information about a faraway place can be obtained from books before a visit is made. Show the children evocative pictures of seaside places where the skies are blue, the sea and sand look inviting and perhaps where there are palm trees and attractive beach huts.

Ask the children what sort of a seaside place they would choose for a holiday. What are the most important features they would want to find? Ask them to close their eyes and imagine their ideal seaside holiday in a distant place.

Discuss the children's requirements. Do they generally agree? Perhaps some children are happy with the sun, sand and sea. Others might like more adventurous activities and need places to explore, to fish, perhaps go out in a boat or play at a water park. Compile a list of the features the ideal resort should have, which the children will be able to refer to later. For example: a harbour, a lighthouse, rocky pools, cliff-top walks, a children's swimming pool, hotels, restaurants.

Suggest the children write a report about a seaside place they would like to visit. Encourage them to look for an ideal destination in the travel brochures and be prepared to include as much detail as possible about their chosen holiday. Read out some extracts from the brochures to suggest how their information can be arranged.

Some children can find out in which country the place is and pinpoint it on the large map.

Recording
Using travel brochures and other information they have remembered, ask the children to write their report, describing a place they would like to visit and what is so attractive about it. They should record where the place is, how they might travel there and then describe how they expect to enjoy themselves during their holiday.

Differentiation
Children:
■ find out about a faraway seaside place and provide reasons why they would like to visit
■ collect information in order to write a report about a faraway seaside place and provide reasons why they would like to visit
■ collect detailed information about a faraway seaside place, locate the place on a map, write a report on its features and provide reasons why they would like to visit.

Plenary
Point out that the children have found out a great deal of information about a distant seaside place. Ask some of them to read extracts from their reports for the rest of the class to consider. Would other children like to go to these places too?

Display
Develop a travel agent theme. Add the children's work from this activity to the holiday brochure. Mark some of the destinations on the large map.

ACTIVITY 4

HOLIDAY WEATHER

GEOGRAPHY

Learning objective
To be aware of the effect of weather on people and their surroundings, and to record their feelings in a poem.

Resources
Pictures showing different weather conditions at the seaside; board or flip chart; paper; pencils and crayons.

Activity
Refer to activity 1 if appropriate, and establish that one of the reasons people go abroad to take their holidays is the weather. Ask what sort of weather holidaymakers like best of all if they are going to the seaside. They want warmth and lots of sunshine so they can wear their shorts, T-shirts and swimsuits and take part in all kinds of outdoor activities in an enjoyable way. Point out that in some other countries people can expect this type of weather nearly all the time. Ask if any of the children know any places where the weather is usually warm

and sunny (for example, the Canaries and Balearics, the West Indies, countries in north Africa, Florida). Has anyone been there?

Then talk about the weather in this country. Mention the warm summer days we often have and ask the children how they feel when the sun shines. However, we often have rainy days in summer and it can sometimes be quite cold. How do we feel when we are on holiday and it is wet and cold? Does the weather sometimes spoil a holiday?

Point out that seaside places can often be very breezy because the wind can sweep across the sea. Places with cliffs and mountains can also be windy. Encourage the children to share their experiences of strong winds and storms, perhaps when they were on a boat or up a mountain. Did they enjoy the experience or were they frightened? Ask the children if they think people who live in windy places get used to it. Talk about breezes being useful for sailing and kite flying.

Take this opportunity to remind the children about avoiding the strong rays of the sun. Ask them to tell each other what precautions are needed to prevent skin from burning. Talk about the importance of wearing a sun hat, using plenty of sunscreen and playing in the shade, perhaps under a beach umbrella. As a contrast, ask the children to describe their wet weather kit, which might include rain hat and coat, umbrella and wellington boots. Ask how people can keep out of the wind. Talk about finding shelter where the wind is not as strong.

Ask the children to think of words that describe three days of weather: an ideal sunny day, a wet day and a windy day. Group these words under appropriate headings on the board. Encourage the children to use the words to build up phrases that can develop into a poem about how people feel and behave on holiday depending on the weather. Help the children to write the first few lines of each verse (see left, for example).

The lines of the poem can be short and continue at random, or describe in order the events in a day.

Recording

Ask the children to create a poem of three parts. Encourage them to mention events and activities that were enjoyed and to try to include their feelings for three days of different weather. Ask the children to print or write out their poems neatly, decorating the verses according to the weather described.

Differentiation

Children:
■ with help put together phrases to describe the effects of different types of weather on holidaymakers at the seaside
■ provide phrases to create a poem that describes the effects of different types of weather on holidaymakers at the seaside
■ provide imaginative phrases to create a poem that contrasts the effects of different types of weather on holidaymakers at the seaside.

A sunny day
Hurrying to the beach
Slopping on the sunscreen
Digging in the sand
Building a huge castle
Paddling in the sea
Smiling and laughing

Plenary

Ask the children to read out some of their verses and comment on the effectiveness of their descriptions. Emphasise lines that are evocative of days by the sea.

Display

Using the title 'Holiday weather', display the children's poems. If space is limited, collect the poems into a book for the library area.

Music

FOCUS

MUSIC

MUSIC
- **sounds and music reflecting different landscapes**
- **seaside sounds**
- **variations in sounds**
- **sources of sounds**
- **developing and practising a class composition**

MUSIC

ACTIVITY 1

LANDSCAPE SOUNDS

Learning objective
To recognise how sounds can be used descriptively and how music can describe an environment.

Resources
Recorded sounds representing the town (traffic, voices, a clock chiming), countryside (cows, sheep and birds, a stream rushing) and seaside (waves, pebbles crunching, seagulls); short pieces of music that evoke the different images of town, countryside and seaside; paper; pencils and crayons.

Preparation
Sequence the sounds to be played immediately one after the other.

Activity
Prepare the children to listen. Make sure they are sitting comfortably and understand that they should listen carefully without any interruptions. Play the three sets of sounds. When they have heard them all, ask the children where they think the sounds were recorded. During the discussion, identify some of the sounds and establish that one group of sounds was in a town or city, another group in the countryside and the third group by the sea. Talk about how the conclusions were reached and which clues helped the children identify the landscapes. Ask which group of sounds best represents the area where the children live. If appropriate, take the children into the school grounds to listen for the sounds of the locality. Notice any periods of silence that might occur and relate this to the locality. If there is not a quiet moment, consider why this is and whether there might be a period of silence at a different time of the day.

In the classroom, tell the children to become quiet and focus on listening again. Play the three pieces of music that represent the three types of landscape. Then ask the children for their first impressions. Are they aware of distinct images at this stage? Play the pieces of music again separately, so the children can discuss each one in turn. What is it about the music that makes them think of each landscape? Can they identify the sounds that indicate a busy place, a tranquil place, a place by the sea? Does the music rely on fast or slow, loud or soft sounds to create the picture? How do the pieces differ?

6

Music

Recording
If appropriate, the children could make a drawing of one or more of the images the music has created for them.

Differentiation
Children:
■ are aware that different sounds and pieces of music can be used to create images
■ are aware that different sounds can be used descriptively and music can be used to represent different images
■ understand how different sounds and music can describe different situations, recognising some of the techniques used to create successful images.

Plenary
Ask the children to provide words that describe the musical images of the town, the countryside and the seaside. Which landscape is best described by slower sounds; which by faster sounds?

MUSIC

ACTIVITY 2

SOUNDS OF THE SEASIDE

Learning objectives
To be aware that words can describe sounds; to use voices to create different sounds.

Resources
Recording of seaside sounds; board or flip chart; paper; pencils and crayons.

Activity
Refer to the previous activity, in which the children identified sounds and music representing different landscapes. Ask the children to focus on the seaside sounds. Perhaps play the seaside sounds again. Then make a list of all the things the children can think of that make sounds in a seaside setting, such as waves, pebbles underfoot, seagulls, donkeys, voices, vehicles, boats/ships and fairground rides. This will be the first column of a chart.

Before asking the children to try out sounds with their voices, make them aware of a signal you will use that will tell them when to stop and listen again. Try an obvious hand signal or a quiet clap to limit the level of sound.

Move on to discussing words that describe the sounds made and add these to a second column on the board. First, ask the children for their suggestions for the sounds of the sea, particularly the waves: *splash, crash, lap, roar, swish*. Encourage the children to repeat the words in a way that reflects their meaning. Practise each word several times, with individuals and groups of children demonstrating. Talk about the words sounding like their meaning. Experiment with other words describing the wave sounds, emphasising and lingering on parts of words such as the *sw* and *sh* of *swish* and sometimes making them sound soft, sometimes getting louder.

Similarly, ask the children to think of words that could sound like people walking on a pebbly beach, crunching their way down to the splashing waves.

Complete the chart, with the children suggesting words for other sounds. Try *mew* for a seagull, *heehaw* for a donkey and any words the children can think of to describe mechanical sounds. Include weather sounds such as the pitter-patter of a shower, the roar of thunder and the moaning of the wind. Consider how people feel when the weather is unpleasant and talk about the effectiveness of the word *shiver*. For voices, include *laughter, shout, cry, buzz* and note those that the children think are onomatopoeic. Analyse some of the words to discover why they are effective. For example, *crunch* and *crash* sound hard and help us to think of pebbles and big waves. Sounds with a blend like *spl* seem softer and gentler. Underline the parts of the words the children think should be emphasised.

Let pairs of children practise using their voices to experiment with onomatopoeic words.

Recording
Ask the children to make a list of their favourite onomatopoeic words, using crayons to highlight the effective parts of each word. They could use larger, heavier print to emphasise the letters that make the most impact.

Differentiation
Children:
■ are aware that there are words which suggest the sounds they describe and can use these words effectively
■ know that there are words which suggest the sounds they describe, recognise why these words are successful and use them effectively
■ make a collection of onomatopoeic words, understand why they are successful in describing sounds and use them effectively.

Plenary
Ask the children to remind each other of some onomatopoeic words. Ask for their favourites. Discuss how useful these words are when describing different scenes.

Display
Print out a selection of onomatopoeic words, emphasising the parts that are most effective. Include these in the seaside display begun in section 2.

ACTIVITY 3

CHANGING SOUNDS

MUSIC

Learning objective
To experiment with creating and changing sounds.

Resources
Recording equipment; paper; pencils and crayons.

Preparation
If appropriate, record some examples of onomatopoeic words and descriptive phrases, some of which include recognisable changes, such as getting louder and softer, faster and slower, higher and lower.

Activity
Remind the children of their explorations of onomatopoeic words. Explain that these words can be even more effective if certain changes are made. Provide some examples using your own voice (perhaps recorded) so that the children might suggest that the sound could be made louder or softer, slower or faster. Discuss situations where sounds will get louder and

softer, such as walking towards the splashing waves and away again, footsteps crunching along a pebbly beach and into the distance, or a seagull calling nearby and then from a distance.

Continue with examples where the tempo changes. Perhaps the waves wash up the beach quickly and move back slowly, a person walks slowly and then more quickly across the pebbles, or the rain starts slowly and then becomes a downpour. Encourage the children to imagine these scenes, perhaps closing their eyes to help them listen more carefully.

Encourage the children to sing a familiar seaside song, sometimes faster, sometimes slower, perhaps higher and lower, louder and quieter.

Next, ask the children to work in pairs to create a short sequence that describes a scene at the seaside. They should use their voices and appropriate words to explore an image that others will recognise. They should try to make changes so that their sequence includes variations: loud and quiet, slow and fast, long and short. Tell them that you will record their efforts so they can hear for themselves how effective their ideas have been.

Play the sequences and discuss the images created. Sometimes the pairs can introduce their sounds and tell the others what to expect. For other sequences, play the recording first and ask what images come into the children's minds. Talk about successful examples as well as where improvements might be made: perhaps changes in tempo or dynamics need to be more emphatic.

Recording
It might be useful if the children attempt a script for their sequence, using symbols, code words and colours. This will help them to remember which part each of them played in the sequence, what words were used and when the changes occurred, and will be useful if performing it again.

Differentiation
Children:
■ are aware that changes can be made to develop an image created by sounds
■ imitate sounds to create an image, making effective changes in dynamics, tempo and pitch
■ put together sounds to develop an image, understanding how changes in dynamics, tempo and pitch can create an effective sound picture.

Plenary
Comment on how well the children worked to create their images and how you enjoyed listening to them. Point out improvements that might be made in future performances.

ACTIVITY 4

SOURCES OF SOUND

MUSIC

Learning objective
To explore and practise playing sounds made by different instruments.

Resources
A range of simple instruments that can be used to make sounds of the seaside.

Preparation
Select instruments that the children can use to portray the seaside sounds discussed in previous activities. Before the activity, arrange the instruments where they can be seen and are easily accessible.

Activity

Point out that the children have been using only their voices to create seaside sounds so far and that this has been very effective. Now it is time to look at other ways of making these kinds of sounds.

Show the children the range of instruments and ask them to think about which ones could make the sounds and words they associate with the seaside. For instance, which instrument would the children think of using if they wanted to create the sounds of the splish-splashing of the waves? Ask for their ideas and then ask a child to demonstrate with one of the instruments. Is the sound what they expected? Try another suggestion for the same sound. Compare the effectiveness of two or more instruments. Can the children think of ways of improving the sounds by making changes in the way the instrument is played? They might want to use different movements, beaters and so on. They could try making louder or softer sounds, play faster or more slowly, or alter the duration for different effects.

Choose another image, such as walking on different surfaces – a pebbly beach, a hard footpath, a sandy beach. Ask for the children's suggestions for instruments to create these scenes and try out their ideas as before. Suggest improvements where appropriate. Emphasise differences in dynamics and tempo and how these changes can affect the image created. Demonstrate the impact of a pause, and what a period of silence might convey.

Consider the instruments that suit weather sounds at the seaside. Which would demonstrate the sound of rain, or perhaps a storm with thunder? What are the children's suggestions for sunshine?

Provide opportunities for all the children to experiment with instruments and to make sounds that imitate the sounds of the seaside.

Differentiation

Children:
- select instruments to represent specific sounds, experimenting with dynamics and tempo
- select different instruments to create a range of sounds, exploring dynamics, tempo and duration of sound
- show imagination and skill when selecting instruments to create specific sounds, exploring dynamics, tempo and duration.

Plenary

Remind the children how instruments as well as voices can produce sounds to represent different seaside scenes.

ACTIVITY 5

PUTTING SOUNDS TOGETHER

MUSIC

Learning objective

To experiment with combining different sounds.

Resources

The collection of instruments used in the previous activity; recording equipment; paper; pencils and crayons.

Activity

Remind the children that they have experimented with making seaside sounds using their voices and also using a range of instruments. Now they can try combining these different sounds. Explain that the children will work in pairs to create an interesting seaside image;

Music

one person will provide voice sounds while the other will produce sounds made by an instrument. Provide some ideas if necessary. The scene could involve a walk along the beach down to the sea, or lying in the shade with eyes closed listening to the sounds all around. Suggest that some sounds are close by and others are in the distance. Perhaps the children might like to include some seaside weather sounds in their sequence.

Ask the children to plan their seaside sound picture. First, they should consider what their sequence will describe. If appropriate, encourage them to make notes to focus their thinking and help them remember what they have decided. Next, they should think about the instrument that will produce the sounds they require and the part the voice will play. Remind the children about the impact silence can make during a musical sequence. Suggest they try to include a pause or two among their sounds.

After thinking time, let the pairs of children practise their ideas. Where necessary, help them to focus on their task, providing subtle advice and encouragement. Talk to them about changing the dynamics and tempo of their sequence, about the effect of having a silent moment. Bring the children together and ask pairs to perform their sequences. Encourage some to introduce and describe their ideas; others can perform first so that the rest of the class can form their own first impressions and decide on the theme. Comment on particularly effective ideas and point out ways where improvements could be made. If appropriate, record the children as they perform and encourage positive feedback.

Recording
Some children might want to write a simple script as before to record their ideas. Point out that others might find the script helpful if they would like to try to copy their sequence.

Differentiation
Children:
■ with help, create an image that can be interpreted with an instrument and voice
■ devise and interpret an image successfully, using voice and a carefully selected instrument
■ explore the possibilities of using different sound sources; devise and practise an imaginative sound sequence that combines voice and instrument.

Plenary
Emphasise the development of using voices together with an instrument. Comment on successful performances and provide encouragement for future activities.

ACTIVITY 6

CLASS COMPOSITION – PLANNING

MUSIC

Learning objective
To provide ideas for planning a class composition.

Resources
Board or flip chart.

Preparation
Have a clear idea of how the planning will proceed. The experience and abilities of the children as well as the time available for planning and practice will determine the detail of the composition. A simple sequence can include variation of tempo, dynamics, and pitch, as well as an effective silence.

Start by outlining a brief story sequence with a beginning, a middle and an end, so the children are aware of the framework early in the planning. Add some detail to develop an interesting sequence of events. Decide which sounds will be represented. Consider any background or distant sounds that can be added to develop the seaside theme. Decide where variations of tempo, dynamics and pitch can be introduced for effect. Pinpoint a place for a pause. Introduce weather sounds.

Activity

Talk about the children's efforts to create a short seaside sound sequence. Explain that using their experience and newly learned skills they can all work together to produce a class composition that will describe a seaside scene. Everyone will be involved in making a seaside story in sound.

Discuss how the story sequence might develop. Perhaps referring to ideas from activity 5, ask the children to help you with the plan, which will need a beginning, a middle and an end. Start with a general title such as 'On the beach', 'A day by the sea' or 'Seaside games'. Divide the board into three areas for beginning, middle and end, and ask for the children's suggestions for each part, for example: *Arrive at the beach and play on the sand. Walk down to the sea. Return, pack up and go home.* Discuss each section, reminding the children that sounds will tell the story and will need to be clear and accurate. Add sound words appropriate to each section.

Beginning: Arriving at the beach can involve walking down steps before reaching the sand. What are the children's ideas for these contrasting sounds? Suggest the steps are hard and probably made of concrete, so walking down the steps will make a distinctive sound. A softer sound is needed for walking on the sand. Talk about which games might be played on the beach: perhaps the sound of a ball hit by a bat, or sounds of digging.

Middle: Footsteps over shingle down to the sea. The sound of the waves will get louder, perhaps there will be seagulls calling.

End: A walk back over crunching pebbles and shells, perhaps back over sand and up the steps.

Go over the framework and ask the children where other background sounds could be added to make the sound story more interesting. They might suggest distant fairground sounds, other families playing and chatting or a donkey braying.

Ask the children where they will need to make the sounds louder or softer. Use a coloured pen to indicate these changes on the plan. Use different colours to denote changes of tempo and pitch as appropriate. Decide and mark where in the story a moment of silence might be effective. Perhaps prompt the children to make the ending more dramatic by introducing a rain shower. Only include as much detail in the plan as you think the children can cope with.

Perhaps rethink the title in the light of the planning ideas; ask for the children's suggestions for a more imaginative or appropriate idea.

Differentiation

Children:
■ follow the planning procedure, making some contributions to a class composition
■ understand the need for planning and provide relevant ideas for a class composition
■ provide relevant and imaginative ideas for planning all aspects of a class composition.

Plenary

Summarise the plan and suggest the children begin to think of the instruments and voice sounds that might be used.

© Getty Images/Mel Yates

6

Music

MUSIC

ACTIVITY 7

CLASS COMPOSITION – CHOOSING AND PRACTISING SOUNDS

© Bubbles/Jennie Woodcock

Learning objective
To use sounds and select instruments for a class composition.

Resources
The plan of the composition from the previous activity; a range of instruments; recording equipment; small cards or large Post-it Notes; Blu-Tack; paper; pencils and crayons.

Activity
Remind the children of the plan they helped to devise during the previous activity, briefly summarising the pattern of the sequence. Tell them that the next step is to plan which vocal and instrumental sounds to use in the piece.

Start with the beginning section of the plan and consider the sounds that need to be made. Which instruments do the children think will interpret each of the sounds of this part of their story? Write the suggestions on cards and attach them to the plan with Blu-Tack or on Post-it Notes. Decide if any of the sounds required are best made vocally. Ensure the children plan to use both vocal and instrumental sounds.

Consider again where variations in tempo, dynamics and pitch will be effective, and if a short silence is to be part of this section. Talk through the proposed sequence and suggest overlapping of sounds. Point out that as one sound is fading away another might begin.

Repeat this process for the middle and end sections, the children using their previous experience to choose instruments and decide upon effective vocal sounds.

Recording
If appropriate, ask the children to draw some of the instruments and write words to describe the sounds they will make in the piece. They could choose an instrument from each section of the composition.

Differentiation
Children:
■ recall some internalised sounds when selecting instrumental and vocal effects for a class composition
■ recall internalised sounds accurately when selecting instrumental and vocal effects for a class composition
■ recall a range of sounds accurately and imaginatively when selecting instrumental and vocal effects for a class composition.

Plenary
Point out that the children have used their knowledge and previous experience of instruments and vocal range to choose sounds for the class composition.

ACTIVITY 8

MUSIC

CLASS COMPOSITION – REHEARSAL

Music

Learning objective
To practise vocal and instrumental sounds.

Resources
A collection of instruments; recording equipment.

Preparation
Decide on the procedure for a practice session. Perhaps divide the class into three groups, each concentrating on one section of the composition.

Activity
Explain to the children that now is the time to put the plan into action and try out the seaside composition. Tell groups which sounds you would like them to practise. Introduce a code of behaviour for the practice session so that everyone has the best chance of making a good effort.

Encourage the children to relate their sounds closely to the sound story they have planned. They could think in terms of composing a string of words or a sentence in sound. Remind them that the words are described by voice and instrument and might need to change, becoming faster, slower, higher, lower, louder or quieter to achieve the best effects.

After a practice session, bring the children together to perform and listen to each other's efforts. Encourage the listeners to remain quiet and still. Perhaps make recordings at this stage.

Comment on the children's performances. Listen to and comment on the recordings if appropriate. Ask the children to listen out for interesting and effective changes in tempo, dynamics and pitch. Praise especially effective vocal and instrumental arrangements. Discuss where improvements can be made, such as more subtle or more dramatic variations, depending on the effect required.

Ask the children to help decide upon the most effective combination of sounds for the class composition. Does it represent the story? Is there enough contrast between the three sections? How will the sections be linked together?

Perhaps write a simple script with symbols and colours that will show the children when they need to contribute their sounds. Indicate where sounds will overlap and where any silent moment will come. Ensure each pair or group of children feels valued and understands their part in the final performance.

When the sequence has been decided, allow the groups to practise their parts individually once again, thinking about their part in the whole sequence.

Differentiation
Children:
■ practise vocal and instrumental sounds as part of a class sequence
■ practise vocal and instrumental sounds, considering variations where appropriate, and understand their part in a class composition
■ with skill and imagination, practise vocal and instrumental sounds, including variations where appropriate, and understand their part in a class composition.

Plenary
Ask the children to try to remember their part in the class composition in preparation for the performance. Praise any special efforts relating to musical skills and suitable behaviour.

MUSIC

Music

ACTIVITY 9

CLASS COMPOSITION – PERFORMANCE

Learning objectives
To use vocal and instrumental sounds appropriate to a class composition; to take part in a performance.

Resources
Planning sheet from the previous activity; the collection of instruments; recording equipment.

Preparation
Organise the instruments so that they are easily accessible. Decide how the children will be positioned and what they will do with their instruments when not performing. Decide if individual children or groups will need further practice time before they all work together.

Activity
Explain that you are now going to put together all the sounds to create the sound story about the seaside. Show the children the script and make sure they know at which point they need to participate. Remind them of any code that uses colours, names or symbols that will help them.

Point out that you will 'conduct' the children as they perform, using gestures rather than words to guide them through their performance. Explain that the performance will be recorded so that the children can hear it afterwards for themselves.

After the first run through, comment on the success of the composition. Play the recording and ask the children to suggest where any last improvements might be made. Perhaps a more gradual changeover would be effective, an extra background sound would enhance the story, or a neater ending could be devised.

Put the improvement ideas into practice as a final performance and record this too.

Consider the success of the new version. Ask the children for their opinions of the class sound composition. Did they enjoy playing in and then hearing the final performance? Are they proud of their efforts? What have they learned or discovered as they worked towards the finished story? What might they think of doing another time in the light of what they have experienced? What other themes might be chosen for a class composition?

If appropriate, the children can perform their composition for another class, as part of an end of term concert or during a visit to school by parents or governors. Perhaps the recording can be played for visitors or for the children themselves to appreciate again, particularly when doing other work on the seaside.

Differentiation
Children:
■ rehearse and take part in performing a class composition
■ rehearse and perform a class composition, offering suggestions for improvements
■ rehearse and show imagination and skill when performing a class composition, offering relevant suggestions for improvements.

Plenary
Praise the efforts of the children in working towards and performing their class composition. Point out what an achievement it has been and how much they have learned about sounds, especially those relating to the seaside.

CURRICULUM LINKS ages 5–7: The seaside

Display

It is important to display as much as possible of the children's topic work relating to the seaside. Making their efforts available for others to see not only adds value and prestige to what the children have achieved, but also emphasises the importance of the information they have discovered or collected, the ideas they have had and the explorations they have made.

If children know their work is valued and available for others to examine and discuss, they will take care over the presentation, and at this stage the habit of always producing their best efforts is encouraged.

Individual presentation

Collect each child's individual paper work – drawings, completed worksheets, written accounts and reports and so on – and present them together in a folder or as a booklet, which they can personalise and show to each other and their families. If necessary, any pieces of work needed for classroom display can be photocopied for the children.

Provide photocopies of the photographs, postcards and artefacts such as tickets to include with the children's work, along with photographs of, for example, the children interviewing their visiting speaker.

Classroom display

Collect and present artefacts representing the seaside to enhance the display of information and stimulate the children's work from the start.

It can be useful to display each child's work relating to any specific activity in a temporary way, perhaps with Blu-Tack, so that discussion and evaluation can take place and the work can be admired. At this stage, make sure the work is displayed on a level where it can easily be seen by all the children. Where appropriate, photocopy and enlarge examples of individuals' work to use with a particular display.

If space is limited in the classroom, extend displays into corridors or the school hall. The hall or foyer may be particularly suitable for displaying the children's travel brochure and posters.

Frequently refer to the displays as the topic develops, reminding the children of the different elements of their work and the progress they are making, and making links and connections across different areas of the topic.

The areas of work that arise from the activities in this book can usefully be displayed as separate but linked displays. For instance:

- Introducing holidays
- The survey
- Mapwork
- Different environments/comparing localities
- The seaside
- The seaside in the past
- The travel agent

Introducing holidays
Arrange the timeline from section 1, together with books, pictures and suitable artefacts relating to festivals and seasons. Include the children's work from activities 1 and 2 as well as the collections of holiday/school items.

The survey
To emphasise the importance of the survey, try to display the work associated with data collection as well as the results in a prominent place where others can see it. Perhaps an entrance hall or corridor would be suitable.

Display

Mapwork

As using maps and developing mapping skills is an essential element of geography, it is appropriate to devote a special display to work with maps. The display of maps should evolve as the work develops. Encourage the children to think of the area as a map workshop.

Start with a large, simple map of the British Isles that could be an outline you have traced and cut out (or enlarged from photocopiable page 18). By arranging a cut-out on a blue background to represent the sea, the children will be more aware of the distinction between land and sea. Make detachable labels to identify Scotland, England, Wales and Ireland. Use different coloured stickers to represent the locations of towns, areas of countryside and seaside places, as discussed in section 1, activity 4. Display nearby a satellite photograph of the British Isles and make atlases and a globe accessible for the children to examine.

As the activities progress, add further seaside places to the large map and print out statements relating to the positions of the children's locality and the nearest seaside places. Aerial photographs can be incorporated with the mapwork display as well as the enlarged map from section 3, activity 2. Add maps of the world as the work is extended in section 5. Use examples of the children's mapwork to add to the map workshop.

Different environments

Represent the different environments of town, countryside and seaside in three distinct areas (perhaps three circles), creating montages of drawings, symbols, photographs, and printed names relating to specific areas (for example, London, Lake District, Llandudno) and using geographical vocabulary. Use colour to accentuate the differences and include children's work as well as maps from section 1, activity 4.

Later, use the work from section 3 where comparisons are made with the home locality and the seaside to add to this display.

The seaside

Bring a flavour of the seaside to the classroom by creating a distinctive display to include artefacts, modern souvenirs, postcards, photographs, posters and holiday guides as well as the children's work. Perhaps produce a frieze with a painted background of beach huts, sand and sea, and distant cliffs on which to display information. Picture story books are a good source of ideas. Use beach toys, swimwear, sunglasses, sun hats, sunscreen bottles and so on to extend the theme. The children will enjoy contributing suitable items. Try to include some references to good seaside weather.

The seaside in the past

Create a backdrop representative of the seaside of past times, particularly during the era of the children's parents or grandparents. Perhaps use ideas from old posters or advertising material. Use historical artefacts and any photographs taken during the visitor's talk in section 4, activity 3. Try to show through appropriate labelling that the information discovered about the seaside in times past came from different sources. Arrange the children's posters to enhance the display.

The travel agent

Turn a corner of the room into a travel agent's counter. Decorate it with posters, brochures, maps, timetables and so on. Encourage pairs or groups of children to take turns to role-play the provision of a travel service for others. They can use the work that develops from section 5.

Music

Any written work or pictures arising from the music activities can be incorporated into appropriate displays. Arrange the instruments and make labels to demonstrate the seaside sounds each instrument was used for. Write out the children's favourite onomatopoeic words and include them in the seaside display.

Assessment

At the end of the topic *The seaside*:

GEOGRAPHY

■ Can the children talk about places they would like to visit?
■ Can they use a map of the British Isles as well as atlases to locate familiar places?
■ Do they know that there are different types of environment?
■ Did they, with help, design and carry out a survey?
■ Did they use a range of resources to describe what it is like at the seaside?
■ Can they identify natural and human features of the seaside?
■ Can they recognise buildings and land use specific to the seaside?
■ Have they used knowledge and awareness of their own locality to compare it with that of the seaside?
■ Do they use a range of geographical vocabulary?
■ Are they aware of some seaside places around the world?
■ Can they communicate information as a poem?

HISTORY

■ Are the children aware of some of the reasons why we have holidays?
■ Do they know the key holiday times of the year?
■ Did they use photographs to discover clues about the past?
■ Do they recognise features and activities that indicate the past?
■ Could they recall information from their past?
■ Do they use vocabulary relating to the passing of time?
■ Can they make comparisons between holidays of today and of the past?
■ Do they know that there are different ways of finding out about the past?
■ Can they recognise that some things change while others stay the same?
■ Can they identify objects belonging to the past?

MUSIC

■ Do they appreciate that music can describe different environments?
■ Are they aware that words can describe sounds?
■ Do they understand that sounds can be changed?
■ Did they explore changes of tempo, pitch, timbre and dynamics?
■ Do they know that there are different sound sources?
■ Do they understand ways in which sounds can be combined?
■ Did they explore and practise sounds made by different instruments?
■ Did they take part in choosing and practising sounds for a class composition?
■ Have they rehearsed and taken part in a performance?

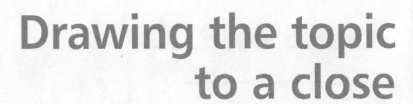

Drawing the topic to a close

Look back with the children over the work they have done on the seaside and highlight any special incidents and achievements. Point out how much they have learned, all the new things they have discovered, the information that has been collected and the enjoyment they have had. Remind them about the visitor who came to talk, artefacts they have seen and experiences they have shared. Emphasise how much more familiar the children now are with different places in this country and around the world, and what the seaside was like in the past. Point out that using maps and comparing different parts of the country are elements of geography, and that by using a range of methods to find out about the past they are discovering history. Talk about the children's musical achievements and the important part the class composition has contributed to the seaside theme.

Ask the children which parts of the topic they have enjoyed the most and which piece of work they are most proud of.

Arrange a simple event as a finale. Perhaps the children can describe their seaside experiences to the rest of the school during an assembly. Include pieces of information, poems, posters and elements of music in this. Invite parents/carers and other family members into the classroom to look at the children's achievements. Suggest pairs of children act as guides and talk about the different aspects of their work.